the empty honour board

the empty honour board

a school memoir

martin flanagan

VIKING
an imprint of
PENGUIN BOOKS

VIKING

UK | USA | Canada | Ireland | Australia
India | New Zealand | South Africa | China

Viking is part of the Penguin Random House group of companies
whose addresses can be found at global.penguinrandomhouse.com

Penguin
Random House
Australia

First published by Viking in 2023

Cover images by Anah Olsen/EyeEm/Getty Images, Pongstorn
Pixs/Shutterstock and h.yegho/Shutterstock
Cover design by Alex Ross Creative
Typeset in 12/16.5 pt Bembo MT Pro by Post Pre-press Group, Australia

Printed and bound in Australia by Griffin Press, an accredited
ISO AS/NZS 14001 Environmental Management Systems printer

 A catalogue record for this
book is available from the
National Library of Australia

ISBN 978 0 14377 913 1

penguin.com.au

We at Penguin Random House Australia acknowledge that Aboriginal and
Torres Strait Islander peoples are the Traditional Custodians and the first
storytellers of the lands on which we live and work. We honour Aboriginal and
Torres Strait Islander peoples' continuous connection to Country, waters, skies
and communities. We celebrate Aboriginal and Torres Strait Islander stories,
traditions and living cultures; and we pay our respects to Elders past and present.

'There's a tendency, particularly in our media world, for everything to be binary: good, bad, yes, no, up, down. And we found Hemingway tantalisingly complicated, which is what we like, because it is faithful to human beings.'

American film-maker Ken Burns on why he made a
documentary on writer Ernest Hemingway

'No-one remembers Paul McMahon. Everyone remembers Rinso.'

Paul McMahon, 2023

For Polly

Who stuck with me through the madness

Thank you

I have a lot of friends to thank for helping me write this book. I say to them what Cathy Freeman said to her friends after she won gold at the Sydney Olympics: 'You know who you are.'

I particularly want to thank my publisher, Nikki Christer, who made me think the whole book anew, and my editor, Patrick Mangan, who tested me the whole way.

Introduction

I was warned against writing this.

A novelist declared it an act of insanity. I think he saw the whole exercise as providing my enemies with a map of my inner worlds. But novelists camouflage their inner worlds and call it art. I'm a journalist. My job is mapping the rough, incomplete terrain of human experience.

Another warning came from a man I had long respected. He said, 'You don't want to go stirring up that shit again.'

As he'd seen a lot of shit in his childhood, I thought long and hard on what he said. I could easily come away with shit on myself. This is another realm of storytelling we're entering, talking about events that happened 50-odd years ago involving three molten forces – sex, religion and adolescence. I know that period shaped me like an ocean shapes a coastline, and I gather it shaped others as much or more. But no two cliffs are the same, no two bays ...

By the time you get to my age – 67 at the time of writing – people's sense of their personal history has taken a mythological turn. Most of us cling to the notion that there is meaning in our lives and, whether we know it or not, arrange the furniture in our minds – our memories – accordingly. We acquire a personal mythology, and personal mythologies, when they clash, can do so violently. This is a region where demons lurk.

Howard Goldenberg is a writer I admire. He's an Orthodox Jew and doctor of medicine born in rural New South Wales. Howard has spent the past 20 years doing locums in remote Aboriginal communities and places like the Christmas Island detention centre. He writes about his experiences in a way that is compassionate, while also observing his professional discipline as a trained observer. Howard read an early manuscript of this book and was an enthusiast for getting it published. I was still unsure. However, he did suggest the book should come with a warning. Howard said, 'This will inspire some and strengthen others, but there could also be others it will send into a downward spiral.'

I hereby issue that warning but state that my aim in writing this is to be uplifting. Why do I choose to be uplifting? Because I can.

I attended a Catholic boarding school in Tasmania from 1966 to 1971. Three of the 12 priests on the staff when I arrived have since gone to prison for sexual crimes committed while I was there, and allegations have been publicly directed against others. Further sexual abuse cases occurred at the school after I left, so that as it now stands six former staff members have been sent to jail.

Throughout 2018 and 2019, a stream of claims by former students, some with names, some anonymous, began appearing on the ABC Tasmania website, in a series of stories written by journalist Henry Zwartz. Each disclosure took me back to a time in my life when I thought I inhabited a concrete reality. Now that concrete reality was bending and breaking like buildings in an earthquake. Then, in June 2019, the local parish priest, Father John Girdauskas, came out and said he had been sexually abused by a priest while a student at the school in the 1970s. My eldest brother, Pat, a phlegmatic bloke who attended the old school from 1960 to '65, emailed me: 'Bloody Hell! What next?'

At one stage I was approached by a journalist for an interview. I declined. If I were to speak publicly about my schooldays, I wanted total control over what I said. I didn't want what I had to say being swallowed up into someone else's narrative – particularly someone else who wasn't there when it happened. This isn't just any story to me. This is a primal story, one that unlocks doors into an inner world otherwise kept private.

The reason the journalist approached me, I assumed, was because he'd learned I gave evidence against one of the priests sent to prison. I was 16 at the time the incident occurred and school vice-captain. My statement to the police described being led by a kid at night to where a 12-year-old stood shaking and shuddering in his pyjama trousers. He turned and showed me a spray of semen up his back. That was 1971. Around 30 years later, I got a phone call from the police in the Tasmanian town where the old school sits. I'd always half-expected the call, having done a law degree at university. I knew the difference between evidence and hearsay – what I had seen was evidence. Agreeing to testify was the easy part.

★

It's a very serious matter to give evidence against someone that will send them to prison and destroy their reputation. Being a journalist has taught me how unreliable memory is – how, when you return to stories you wrote years before, you inevitably find that while you remember certain particulars of the story clearly and accurately, there are details you have invented and/or omitted. Basically, we fashion our experience into stories we can live with. We decorate our inner selves as busily as we decorate our houses.

Having zealously avoided colluding with any other potential witness in the case, I asked myself, not once but repeatedly, 'How do I know my memory of that night in 1971 is true?' Eventually, I resolved that if I was asked that question in the witness box, I would reply, 'All I know is that whenever I think of that night, the same memory always appears. The same event, the same faces, all appearing in the same order – it never changes.' I was fortified by the fact that I never woke in the night with one of those jolts of excruciating doubt that has come to me in other cases where memory has been an issue.

For decades I had successfully put the old school out of my mind. In 1989, I met Koori songman Archie Roach and heard first-hand his story of being stolen from his family by the 'authorities' and the lifelong ordeal that followed. Archie's story is epic and privately I made a vow to never complain about the old school again. And I didn't. But the old school kept re-entering my life. There were convictions in three further cases for multiple sexual offences committed at the school after I left (none of the offenders in these three cases were priests, although one had formerly been a deacon). The case I gave evidence in went to court in 2007. The third priest from my time went to trial in 2019.

Also in 2019, Paul O'Halloran came out in the media with his brother Steve. Paul was someone I liked a lot at school – an athletic boy with a gentle nature, curly black hair and a generous laugh. He was popular and good at sport. A decade later, when we were at university together, he played in a Uni footy team I coached that made it to a memorable grand final. Over the next 40 years, we had sporadic contact, during which time he also sat in the Tasmanian parliament as a Green.

The story on the ABC website had a photo of Paul sitting on a couch with his arm around his brother Steve. Steve's the younger brother but in the photo he looked much older. I saw one brother carrying another up their own private Kokoda trail. Both O'Hallorans related sexual incidents with two priests – one priest in common – but Steve's experience had proved much more traumatic. He described an incident with a priest which corresponded to one I had with the same cleric. Paul O'Halloran called on former students to speak out ...

★

Shortly thereafter came the bomb blast, heard around the world, that was the guilty finding against Cardinal George Pell in the Victorian County Court on one count of sexual penetration of a child under the age of 16 and four counts of indecent assault of a child under the age of 16. The guilty finding was subsequently overturned by a unanimous decision of the High Court. Throughout this drama, opinions rained down from all sides with one thing in common – the absolute certainty with which they were expressed.

From voices on the Left came the idea that all priests convicted of sexual offences – indeed, some implied all priests – were career paedophiles. On 1 March 2019, in the Fairfax press, celebrity barrister Geoffrey Robertson attempted a more nuanced view. He wrote: 'The reality is that priests abuse small boys not because they are gay but because they have the opportunity. Most are not even paedophiles, but rather sexually maladjusted, immature and lonely individuals unable to resist the temptation to exploit their power over children who are taught to revere them as the agents of God.'

Robertson was howled down, but the priest I gave evidence against could be well described as a maladjusted, sexually immature, lonely individual. I have no idea as to whether he could be correctly termed 'gay', but what I do know is that he had virtually no possibility of a sexual relationship with a woman given his living circumstances.

Meanwhile, from the Right, came a tweet in support of Pell which described him in reverent terms as a Christian saint. I went to the tweeter's home page and found an elderly, ultra-devout English Catholic whose two other principal interests – beyond waging a war against Pope Francis for attempting to modernise the church – were supporting Brexit and defending Donald Trump. In that trifecta of Trump, Brexit and Pell lies a key to the weirdness of our times.

Behind the issue of what actually went on at my school on an island off the southern coast of the world's most southern continent, global forces were at play – ancient controversies to do with the Catholic Church, the Pope, the authority of priests, celibacy, the Vatican's exclusive maleness and the epidemic of sexual abuse that has followed it around the world. Somewhere inside all of that, being thrown about like a leaf in a storm, was me, my story.

The journalist in me was provoked in a way it hadn't been since the national drama that erupted around Aboriginal footballer and 2014 Australian of the Year Adam Goodes. At that time, opinions rained down with perfect certainty and very quickly the issue had only two sides, two views. We had entered the realm of what is now termed binary thinking, where issues about deeply sensitive subjects like race and sexuality and gender are reduced almost immediately to black-and-white terms. In the process, Goodes's story, an important and difficult one, was obscured and distorted, the only writer who grasped the story in its complexity and full human shape being Indigenous journalist Stan Grant.

So much contemporary media – particularly social media – reduces human dramas to scenarios in which the forces of darkness are pitted against the forces of light. To blackest black and whitest white. The English novelist Graham Greene once wrote that he didn't believe human nature was black and white – he said it was black and grey. I'm more optimistic than that – I've met people with seams of white in the rock of their being.

What I've never met is someone who was pure white. Whose light didn't come with a shadow. Forty years of working in the media tells me the human impulse to idealise and demonise is not much different than it was in the Middle Ages. What's changed, and will keep changing, are the targets.

Someone who knows a whole lot about this is Lindy Chamberlain, the woman demonised as a witch after she claimed her baby had been stolen by a dingo at Uluru in 1980. Australians didn't know, and didn't want to know, the testimony of the Aboriginal people of Mutitjulu at the base of Uluru – that dingoes eat human babies, that there's been a dreaming story running through Uluru saying as much for aeons. Lindy Chamberlain once remarked: 'When big things happen, people want an explanation. If they don't get one, they make it up.' I agree with Lindy.

That's why I came to hunger for something of a documentary nature about places like my old school; something like George Orwell's essay on his boarding school days, 'Such, Such Were the Joys'. What Orwell described was familiar to me, even though our experiences were on opposite sides of the planet, 60 years and two world wars apart. Something about the dynamics of the place he described, not least the psychology of a child in a world saturated with fear, was instantly recognisable to me.

One day I rang my brother Tim and said, 'Doesn't it strike you as strange that lots of people who weren't at our school are certain they know what happened there, and you and I were there and we're not?' He agreed it was strange. And so, hesitantly, I began to write. Why? Because, in the end, that's what writers do.

*

I haven't named the school. The events I describe happened long ago. It ceased being an all-boys' school in 1972, the year after I left. The order of priests who ran it in my day no longer have anything to do with the operation. There are no boarders. While the name of the school will be known to people in the region, this is a book being sold around Australia and possibly overseas.

The old school's honour board doesn't have an entry for my last year. Perhaps it's because the following year the school started a new era by going co-ed, perhaps it's because my last year ended in a scandal. The tide of golden print records the year – 1971 – but after that are empty spaces of varnished wood. The real names in this book are my honour board, although the list, I must add, is far from complete.

I have not named names as comprehensively as some will wish. If I used names in a way that was seriously damaging to reputations, I would be obliged to go through the same long process I went through before giving evidence against the priest. It would mean scrupulously re-examining each event I describe, studying its nuances from every possible angle and then describing the whole matter in a way that accommodated every such nuance. In short, the book would never be written.

This is what might be loosely termed my testimony. Or, to put it in the vernacular: do you want to know what happened at places like the school I went to in the 1960s and '70s? I'll tell you what I know. I speak for no-one but myself.

★

I'm going to try and resist the temptation to describe the old school as a prison. I worked in Hobart's Risdon prison (known simply as Risdon) for a spell in my early 20s – I know the differences and they are harsh. But there are similarities. In 1983, Risdon was flooded by young people from all over Australia protesting the damming of one of the island's last wild rivers, the Franklin. The protest leader, Bob Brown, told me some years later that the protesters who did best inside – who did what prisoners call their 'time' most easily – were the ones who'd been to boarding schools. What those young people had, I imagine, was the habit of mind that comes from having to inhabit the empty cell of self for long periods, from steeling yourself to the knowledge that you can't go home, that you simply have to adapt to the place you find yourself in.

Here is another similarity. The Christmas before I started at the old school, my brother Tim and I were lying on a beach wearing plastic sunglasses we'd bought for two shillings at Coles in Ulverstone. He was 13, I was 10. He told me about the school and made it sound pretty good, but he said there were two rules. Don't dob and don't suck up to authority. When I worked in Risdon prison, I was told the prisoners' code of honour. Don't dob. Don't suck.

If you are to enter the world I am about to describe, you have to understand something that I could never explain to cartoonist John Spooner, with whom I worked for 32 years at *The Age*. Politically, John and I differed so we talked about everything else. He was wont to psychoanalyse me, particularly my relationship with my mother. I was never able to explain to him, try as I might, that his analysis rested on a Freudian assumption that simply didn't apply in my case – the assumption that people are to be understood by their relationships within the family home during their formative years. The reason the assumption didn't apply is because my formative years were spent *outside* the family home. My parents were like two planets in a distant galaxy. In simple terms, they were not there.

Did I blame my parents for not being there? No. The thought never entered my head, not then or later. A few years ago, I came across an English 'Survivors of Boarding School' website. Nearly all the stories were about homesickness. I never got homesick and for that I was grateful. To be heard crying in the night was to risk further humiliation.

Why didn't I get homesick? I once spent an afternoon with Father John Brosnan, the former Pentridge prison chaplain who walked Ronald Ryan, the last man hanged in Australia, to the gallows in 1967. Brosnan told me that on that dreadful walk it was the condemned man who gave him courage and not the other way around. Somewhere in the course of the afternoon we had together, Brosnan also remarked that he was someone who 'doesn't miss people'. So am I. My wife says the fact I don't miss people is an example of how boarding school fucked me.

My dialogue with John Spooner turned at one point to which novel had first impressed itself upon our consciousness. His was *Sons and Lovers* by D. H. Lawrence. Mine was *Lord of the Flies* by William Golding, which I read in my fourth year, when I was 14.

Lord of the Flies is the fictional story of a group of English schoolboys marooned on an island after a plane crash. With no adults around to guide or ameliorate their behaviour, they descend into savagery. What I read made perfect sense to 14-year-old me. For years, I carried in my mind a scene near the end where Ralph, the character who attempts to preserve civilised standards, feels a black weight descend on his mind. It's actually a bit more complex than that in the book, but that's how I recalled it over many years. Why? Because a black weight descended on my mind when I was 13; only the black weight wasn't ultimately caused by something someone did to me. It was caused by something I did to someone else.

★

I once ended up at a dinner table beside one of Australia's most senior female judges. She mentioned that she'd gone to boarding school at the age of four.

'Four!' I cried. 'I went at 10 – that was bad enough.'

She leaned towards me and said with sudden intensity, 'But didn't it make you strong?!'

She was looking at me as I imagine she had looked at many barristers over the years, scrutinising them to see if they were as shallow as they seemed. I had to agree. In 37 years, no-one bent or broke me as a journalist.

I'm not saying I was a great journalist. My idea of a great journalist is Marie Colvin, the war correspondent murdered by the Syrian regime in 2012 for standing with the civilian population of Homs as they were being bombarded by their own government, and telling the world. As a journalist, I was once described as 'a worm working in the mulch of his culture'. It seemed a fair description, but, even so, there were certain lines no-one could push me across, and there were those who tried. I fought to defend my work and put my job on the line when I had to.

★

This book is about describing my schooldays and their impact on my adult life. But I wasn't a blank canvas when I arrived at the school. I had history.

Until I was eight, we lived in the small country town of Longford in northern Tasmania. Longford had a silent hierarchy of place born of the Georgian era. Its two main streets are Wellington Street (after the Duke of Wellington) and Marlborough Street (after the Duke of Marlborough). We lived in William Street, named after William IV, enthusiastic champion of the slave trade.

Longford has oak trees and hawthorn hedges and a sandstone Anglican church that is still the centrepiece of the town. In the 1950s and early '60s, most of the houses had a paddock with a couple of sheep or a horse in them. Twenty miles of placid green plains to the south lay the blue line of mountains known as the Western Tiers. I grew up as happy as a small boy could be.

Dad was the primary-school headmaster and a 'returned soldier'. As a headmaster, he was thorough and diligent, returning to the school each night after tea to do paperwork, since he was also teaching a class. I always liked Dad's style as a man. He didn't try to impress – he was his own person. He didn't say much but what he said always made sense to me. He didn't play with us or read to us or do the things fathers usually get judged by. He was remote like a mountain top. He'd survived a war crime – the building of the Burma Railway with slave labour by the Imperial Japanese Army. Dad was also between Nagasaki and Hiroshima when the atomic bombs went off. He had a lot to think about and spent the rest of his life doing so.

He was physically sick for 15 years after the war and once told me that the month of my birth, February 1955, was his worst. I have thought about that. In 1955, the Soviet Union and its Eastern Bloc allies had just signed the Warsaw Pact, and the Vietnam War was beginning. Dad had enlisted because he believed Hitler was a threat to civilised values and now, 10 years after that world war ended, it must have seemed another was on its way. A friend said to me once, 'We inherit our depressions from our fathers.' Maybe I did.

In Tasmanian terms, Dad had been a sportsman of note before the war – winning the Devonport Gift, running third at Burnie, getting games with North Hobart Football Club when they were the best team in Tasmania. In Longford after the war, he coached an under-age footy team which provided Longford with the bulk of its 1957 state premiership side, a big deal since it meant a team from a small country town had triumphed over the best that the cities of Hobart and Launceston could throw against them.

Through one of those quirks you find in sporting history, Longford also had an internationally recognised motor-racing track, twice hosting the Australian Grand Prix. A lot of my early games had to do with racing cars and motorbikes.

Whitefellas first came to Longford in 1813, dispossessing the Panninher people. One of our convict forebears, Irish Catholic Thomas Flanagan, worked on the Brickendon property on the edge of Longford. Another convict forebear, English nonconformist William Steers, absconded from the nearby Panshanger property, which was owned by the notoriously harsh Joseph Archer, and became a bushranger. When he was recaptured 18 months later with a pistol, he was sent to Port Arthur for 'severe discipline'.

The first book I ever read was Frank Clune's biography of Tasmanian bushranger and escaped convict Irishman Martin Cash. Dad wrote that his father sang Ned Kelly songs in a 'strong unmusical voice'. Dad sang Ned Kelly songs in a strong unmusical voice. Does this relate to boarding school? Maybe.

From the moment I arrived at the old school as a 10-year-old, I understood that this strange new universe I found myself in had two forces or, if you like, two sides. One side were few in number but had the power to impose severe punishments. I was on the other side – the ones who didn't want to get caught. I learned, as we all did, to hiss warnings without moving my lips when a priest appeared unannounced at the back of a room.

The priests represented authority, but, that said, there was an authority they never had over me. I never venerated the church. Its rituals and language were never the poetry of my soul. I couldn't be got that way.

★

Mum and I fought over religion from the time I was six or seven. Our religious war was deeply fought, as all religious wars are, and she was often angry. To me the Catholic Church was a cold grey empty tomb where the words were an inconsequential drone and the costumes were of no more interest than those worn in carnivals or at the circus. I was sacked as an altar boy for inattention. Obviously, I didn't have an intellectual position on the church when I was six and seven. My faith could be likened to a wet Band-Aid – it just kept dropping off. Whatever had caused generations of my forebears to adhere to the Church of Rome had, like Elvis, left the building.

I was never an atheist. Parts of the Jesus story resonated strongly with me. '*Let he who is without sin cast the first stone.*' '*By the fruit of their actions, ye shall know them.*' '*Judge not and be not judged.*' And that haunting cry from the cross: '*My God, my God, why have you forsaken me?*' – which actually made me think there might be some truth in the story. It is such an appallingly human cry.

When my father was in his 90s I put it to him straight: 'Dad, did you ever really believe Catholic dogma?' He replied in his succinct way: 'No. Not really.' Neither did I, Dad. As a kid, I watched you not go to communion or confession each week. You didn't recite any prayers. You just sat at the end of the pew with your thoughts.

As I see family history, this attitude that Dad possessed – and which I believe I inherited from him – came from his grandfather, convict bushranger William Steers, the only one of our convict forebears to have been neither Irish nor Catholic. The first story I heard about William Steers was that, in his later years, he would sit on the woodheap when his family went to church and shout, 'No man stands between me and my God!' Dad's mother was a nonconformist Catholic – she identified, like her Irish mother, as Catholic, but she didn't bow to the authority of the priests when they came round and said her kids had to go to church. You were like her, Dad. I was like you.

★

Mum was a farm girl from Melrose, up the back of Devonport. She loved the place she was from, and had an abundance of stories about it, unlike Dad whose past had to be extracted from him detail by detail. Mum was, first and last, loyal – and, in her early life, her religion and her loyalty were one. She was also highly political. In her later years, she couldn't stand the Liberals and gave them names like 'Fatty' Downer. One of the great joys of my life was watching Mum transition out of the religion she was indoctrinated with as a child into the belief system that was innately hers.

Mum was brave and adventurous, but she married a man who'd had more than enough adventures by the time the war ended. Mum lived through her kids and, as her kids changed, so gradually did she, reclaiming her faith to be what she was, an Australian Catholic with a spirituality that was rooted in a place, the green hills of Melrose, and the people of that place.

Dad was solitary, Mum loved what the Irish call the craic – bright chatter, the sound of a happy room, a rough choir of voices in happy harmony. I rang Mum from football grounds around Australia, plugging her into the excitement of matches I was covering. At a Tiwi match I sat behind the coach so she could get the passion of footy expressed in Tiwi. Every grand final day, I rang her from the MCG and let her tune into the big crowd's oceanic roars.

Mum drove like a rally driver. When we lived in Rosebery she gave a lift out to a young male teacher. Forty years later, at a literary festival where he queued to tell me the story, the former teacher said Mum went into a slide on a wet road coming down a mountain. A ravine beckoned. The man blanched at the memory. He said Mum drove like a champion, going with the slide, not hitting the brakes, accelerating out of it. He had a story about her driving trucks during the war. She didn't drive trucks through the war but, as one of my brothers said, she would have loved to.

In their last decade at home, I'd ring Mum and Dad from Melbourne and we'd have what I called 'three-way turf talk', after a Melbourne racing show that was on radio in my teens. Mum and Dad's phone had two receivers, I'd be at the other end. They were in their 90s by then, had both lost a bit, him through attrition, her through a series of strokes. There were no rules. You said what you liked, went where the impulse took you, any interruption being as valid as the next. It was my life history played as jazz.

★

My big moment with Mum came when I was in my 40s. I drove her up to the north of Tasmania so she could see a dying brother. On the way, we visited her old family farm. It was an eye-dazzlingly beautiful day – clear blue sky, most of northern Tasmania laid out beneath us like a green velvet map, to the south the dark gothic hump of Mount Roland, to the north Bass Strait glittering like a jewel.

A sign on the gate said, 'Trespassers Prosecuted'. Mum opened the gate. 'We're not trespassers,' she said, and walked in.

The weatherboard farmhouse stood old and unpainted, stuffed with hay. It was like seeing a cloth doll with straw where the eyes used to be. But it didn't matter. That's the whole point of this story really – she was at home *in the place*. I watched as she walked among her memories and the air became thick with the presence of her old people.

Mum's from the land and so am I. I am not a man of the land in the sense that a farmer is, but I hold nature's truth to be unarguable. I see a beauty in landscapes that makes me yearn more deeply than I can express to be a painter. Mum and I were split in two by religion; in the place she was from we were one. I wept that day like I've never wept as an adult.

★

When I was eight, Dad was transferred to Rosebery, a mining town on Tasmania's wild West Coast. It was another country. Longford was flat, Rosebery was hemmed in by mountains. It never stopped raining in Rosebery and, instead of green paddocks, there were plains of sodden button grass. There were no oak trees or hawthorn hedges – there was impenetrable rain-forest. It wasn't quiet. The day was punctuated by blasts reverberating from under the ground.

Rosebery didn't have Longford's sense of decorum. I saw a drunk man lying unconscious outside the school and was told matter-of-factly by a kid my age that it was so-and-so's father. The kids were like characters out of *Huckleberry Finn*. Two of them took me tramping through the bush. I nearly stepped on a shiny black snake and was startled by the scream that tore from my throat. I wouldn't be that scared again until Herman, the old school's rector, summoned me to his office in my first year.

Rosebery was lonely. Tim, Pat and Mary were away at school, Richard was only two years old, and my sister Jo was a newborn baby. I was 'the headmaster's son'. There was no TV and only a scratchy radio wave coming over the mountains from Queenstown.

It was during this period that the Archbishop of Tasmania came to Rosebery. He dressed in luscious tones of purple and black and had a baritone voice to

23

match. His sermons were longer than the Nullarbor Plain and his admirers gushed over him. While in Rosebery, he contacted my father and asked with the rhythmic bugle of his voice how Dad thought it looked when one of the town's prominent Catholics sent his son (me) to the government school. Dad replied, 'How does it look when the headmaster of the government school sends his son to the other school in town?'

As Tim said years later, when you've been threatened by guards with bayonets, you're not going to be intimidated by someone wearing the costume of the Papal All-Stars.

Around now, I felt the need to know Dad better. One day we went to the local footy. He barely spoke to me on the way there, on the way back, or during the game. I was left with a sense of absence I found disconcerting. Curiously, this need to know Dad disappeared when I went to boarding school and only returned in my 20s when I was desperately trying to make sense of my world. Any Rosebery kid whose family wanted them to get a full secondary education had to 'go away'. That meant, in my case, winning what was then called a junior state bursary. With Dad's stern tutelage, I did. I remember playing on the floor with my toy racing cars and Mum saying it was time I started putting my toys away, because I was about to become a big boy. One week short of my 11th birthday, I left home. I wasn't close to either of my parents, and was glad enough to go. Sounded like an adventure.

★

My brother Tim likes going places, I like being taken places, so from the start we did lots together. When he started primary school, aged five, he took me, aged three, and I pretty much stayed. That's why I was not only a clear year younger than every other kid in my class at boarding school, I was younger than most of the kids in the year behind me.

Tim was the third kid in the family, I was the fourth. We shared bedrooms over the years and at night we'd lie in the dark and he'd tell me about books and magazines he was reading. There was something about the way he told his stories I could listen to endlessly. Still can. Dad said Tim's the best historian in the family – he never tells you anything without telling you how he knows it, who told him or where he read it. That leaves you to attach what weight you will to the information.

I got my politics from Tim, my sense of history. He, and he alone, encouraged me to write. If I ever didn't have money, he would give me some. If being called 'brother' by Indigenous people has meant a lot to me over the years, it's partly because I had a brother who taught me what the word means.

We don't always get on. About 15 years ago, we

went to Ireland together and were glad enough to part at the end. Having spent the previous 25 years trying to understand the Aboriginal way of seeing the land, as someone with Irish aboriginality I wanted to apply that knowledge to the Irish landscape. I wanted to listen to Irish music; he wanted to listen to talkback radio. He wanted to go places; I was happy to sit in pubs and watch and listen. But we still had plenty of laughs and returned with a bag full of stories.

Tim is much changed from the person he was at school. Back then, he was uptight and rigidly demanding of himself. Two bouts with cancer have given him cause for reflection, but his big change started when he met his wife, Fiona Joske, at medical school. Fiona is brave, cheerful and stoic, and she shares my brother's unlimited enthusiasm for socialising and travel. She's also an atheist, a belief she inherited from her philosopher father. As a kid, Tim was pious. He's highly irreverent now.

Tim's given me more nicknames than I can recall, the first and possibly best being 'Dog'. He's eccentric and has a temper, but it passes quickly and no grudges are held. His phonecalls are him at his comic best and we invariably laugh ourselves silly. There is between us some wicked joke that cannot be captured in words, merely felt like a slippery robber in the night.

The best explanation I have for the joke is a quote of Charlie Chaplin's: In any excess of seriousness lurks the absurd. When I was six Tim and I were altar boys

serving benediction. It was a full-dress performance –
we were wearing black soutanes and white surplices.
The priest, singing unaccompanied in a high wavering
voice, sounded like a turtle being throttled. If there's a
comic frequency in the universe, my brother and I both
hit upon it at that moment, making us shake deliriously
as we fought the impulse to laugh.

A second time it happened was in the maximum-
security yard of Risdon prison. What an ultra-macho
sports event in a prison shares with an altar in a Catholic
church is that it's a total humour-exclusion zone. On
that occasion, the prison's fast bowler was trying to
knock our heads off with short-pitched bowling when
Tim inadvertently brought chaos to proceedings and the
match was transformed into slapstick comedy. A third
time was when I was outside the courtroom waiting to
give evidence against the priest, feeling a bit nervous.
Tim whispered a funny story in my ear about Eric, one
of the scariest priests at school.

It doesn't matter what's happening in the world or
who's doing it, my brother can relate it back to a story
from school. *Remember when*, he'll begin. Some say
our laughter is sick and unfeeling towards the pain of
others. This was the criticism of a story we told one
night about a kid who tried to escape boarding school
by jumping on the back of his parents' car as they drove
off after depositing him at the start of a new term. Mum
and Dad got a few hundred metres down the drive

before Dad glanced in the rear-vision mirror and saw son hanging on to the boot for dear life.

We see the kid the same way we saw Steve McQueen in *The Great Escape*, when he jumped the barbed-wire fence of the German prison camp on a motorbike. The kid's a hero in the Irish sense – his story is told to this day. I tell it. The old school was full of heroes with names like Brushy Matthews, Meno Thompson, Rinso McMahon, not to mention a little kid no-one noticed called Johnny G.

★

The old school had a curious gift for nicknames: Hans Christian Hennessy, Drone Lacey, Elegance Cassidy, Bovine Tierney, God O'Connor, Jazz McKenzie, Runt O'Halloran …

Vox Crockett had a high-pitched voice (Latin *vox*, the voice). Vox's younger brother was Little Vox. There were three Dense Hilliards. Scar was a priest whose face was cratered with acne scars, Toad, a priest who was slightly plump. I invented one nickname – Organ Morgan – and, a few years down the track, was chuffed to find it in one of my very favourite literary works, Dylan Thomas's *Under Milk Wood*.

'Flaps' was passed down the line from Pat to Tim to me. It was an unkind name, based on Pat having protruding ears, but I was glad enough to get it since it meant to some extent I was 'in'. Tim later called one of his dog Flaps to exorcise the name. I never bothered. I've acquired more nicknames over the course of my life than any person I know. I keep them in a drawer and wear them like hats.

One of the names from the old school that Tim and I hold dear is Meno Thompson (pronounced 'Men', as in men, and 'oh!'). Meno, who was also from Rosebery, was the kid the system couldn't break. What's more, the system knew it couldn't break him and so did the kids. Meno had the record for the cuts – that is, slices of the cane across a boy's buttocks. It needs to be noted that, among the boarders, the cuts each kid received were a matter of public record since you wore the bruises on your arse for weeks afterwards and we had open showers – everyone knew the score.

In 2019, a claim was made in the media about a kid at the old school getting over 100 cuts in one week. Not to my knowledge, nor that of my two brothers. Meno got the most cuts in a year, a Bradman-esque 234, an average of around six a week. That would keep your arse looking like a medium rare steak.

Meno was presumed thick, but if I'd found out in later life that he was quite brilliant, I wouldn't have been surprised. He looked like a 1970s avant-garde film director from eastern Europe – pale humour-less face, thick glasses, a weird energy, his own way of dressing. Dead at 19 in a motorbike accident. A legend to me and Tim. Our James Dean, our rebel without a cause.

*

At one level, the jokes about our old school are jokes about a place that desperately wanted the outside world to see it as religious, in the sense of holy, sanctified, uplifted. The difference between appearance and reality is what most comedy pivots on. Add to this an exquisite twist of snobbery. We were a boarding school. We saw ourselves as being on a par with the two boarding schools that catered to northern Tasmania's Protestant elite, Scotch College and Launceston Grammar.

When Grammar boys played footy, they called out to one another like young officers on a military manoeuvre. We didn't talk like that. The Catholic school in Launceston only had day boys, which made them, by definition, common. In fact, ours was the cheapest boarding school in the state. We took kids who'd been expelled from other schools and kids from broken homes who were parked there.

A contingent of Asian students appeared in about my third year to boost school finances. One of them, a chap from Singapore with authoritarian tendencies, became a sergeant in the school cadets. On a bivouac in some nearby ranges, he took out a night patrol that never returned. The next morning a scraggly line of uniformed youths carrying .303 rifles, led by an Asian with sergeant stripes, marched through the small, culturally monotone (that is, white) township of Penguin.

Our school competed in events like the Northern Tasmanian Independent Schools Sports, despite having little or no resources and about as much interest. The sports were televised around the island by the ABC and each year we watched our kids run last in virtually every event. It defined us somehow and fed into the general humour of the place.

We had one distance runner who was like a wind-up toy that ran at one pace and never stopped. I'll call him Tomkinson, after the kid in Michael Palin's *Ripping Yarns* who represents his school in the '30-mile hop'. Each year, the week after the Northern Tasmanian Independent Schools Sports, the rector would stand up at school assembly and read out a letter by someone like a retired colonel, saying how impressed he was by Tomkinson in the 5-mile because he ran out the race, even though the winner had finished some time before and the next event was waiting to start. In this way, Tomkinson became our equivalent of the Unknown Soldier – the moral embodiment of a hopeless cause. I vividly recall when we finally won our first event – Theo Dingjan in the Under 14 high jump, using the old scissor-kick jumping technique.

We were even worse at swimming. A few days before the Northern Tasmanian Independent Schools

Swimming Sports, a priest would appear in the dormitory with a pad, basically press-ganging whoever he
could get to go in events.

*Remember the year they put Paddy Maguire in the high
diving at the Northern Tasmanian Independent Schools
Swimming Sports? Paddy was from Hunter Island in Bass
Strait. Didn't like wearing shoes, became an abalone diver.
Paddy could dive, as in dive off the side of a boat. At the
Northern Tasmanian Independent Schools Swimming Sports,
Paddy, having done his dive, was asked to do a second dive 'of
your own choice'. He did the only other one he knew, running
off the end of the board beating his chest like he'd seen in a
Tarzan movie. Remember?*

★

The school was a two-storey red-brick building that
sat atop a bald green hill denuded of the eucalypts that
once crowned the coastline. Facing the school were the
mostly grey waters of Bass Strait. On days when an east-
erly blew, orange effluent from a nearby tioxide plant
streaked the water. The semi-industrial town the school
bordered had maybe 15,000 people, but was a world
apart. The school's seclusion probably explains a lot that
happened there.

Above the glass doors at the main entrance was the
school crest bearing the letters 'AM', daintily inscribed
with a star above them. They signified 'Ave Maria' ('Hail

Mary'). The order of priests running the school orig-
inated in France after the atheistic revolution of 1789.
The revolution had found its symbolic representation in
images of a half-naked young woman brandishing the
French tri-colour.

The Catholic response was a religious order with a
highly romantic devotion to the mother of Jesus (also
known as the Mother of God and the Virgin Mary).
How this veneration of a female figure was meant to
play out in an all-male school I never understood. I
don't think the priests did either, since I never heard
it discussed. By the time I arrived, Mary was a plaster
statue in the school chapel and not much more.
Diagonally opposite the letters AM on the school crest
was a silver sword with a flash of lightning through it,
like you see on the costumes of American superheroes.
Beneath the crest was the school's Latin motto, '*Diligite
Veritatem*'. In English, 'Love the Truth'.

The priests belonged to an order whose heroes were
French missionaries eaten by cannibals in the South
Pacific. Instead of the exotic South Pacific, this generation of priests found themselves in regional Tasmania.
Instead of being missionaries, they were teaching kids
with no interest in their religious order and, from what
I could see, little interest in their religion beyond identi-
fying as Catholics in much the same way they identified
as Collingwood and St Kilda supporters. And that was
a further cultural barrier for the priests – being from

New South Wales, they didn't understand footy. For some of us, footy was all we understood.

The only company the priests had on that lonely hill were other males. The idea, wholly unbelievable to me now, was that we would live without intimacy, the only intimate relationship on offer being with an invisible deity whose address was given, several times a day, as 'Our Father Who Art in Heaven'.

★

The school building was shaped like a dog's leg with a bend in the middle. The eastern end housed the classrooms, six on top, six on bottom. The western end contained the dormitories, chapel and priests' quarters. There were 80 kids in the junior dormitory where I began, their iron beds about 40 centimetres apart – space enough for a narrow chest of drawers. An industrial concertina curtain separated us from the senior dormitory in which there were another 70, maybe more, kids. In my final years, the senior dormitory was partitioned off at one end to give the 20 or so Year 12 boys a separate space, one of the many perks within the boarding-school system of getting older.

The priests' quarters were on the top floor of an extension built on the western end. Each priest had his own room. That in itself was appealing. The school had no privacy whatsoever. If you were seen sliding out of bed in the morning with a *bone* (an erection), you could have a humiliating nickname for life by lunchtime.

In a world where absolutely nothing was private, the priests' rooms were a privileged space. They had desk lamps that made angled realms of soft light. In a square red-brick school with few aesthetic touches beyond the plaster saints in the chapel, that was something remarkable. You had to ask the dormitory master permission to leave the dormitory at night and visit the priests' quarters. This protocol has since been the subject of court discussions in relation to sex offences committed in the priests' rooms. I never knew permission to be refused. You only went to the priests' rooms after you had readied for bed which meant changing into pyjamas.

I wish to emphasise that my boarding-school story is really two stories – the first three years being one story, the second three another. In fact, each of my six years was distinct in character. Each was a separate drama and, in my sixth and final year, I had what is proverbially known as a ball: drinking, smoking, nicking off at night and visiting girls in the town, hitch-hiking from one end of the island to the other. My parents hardly knew what I was doing and, for significant periods, neither did the school. I was free as a bird, happy as a lark, any flying metaphor will do.

★

My first year was 1966. I'm struck now by how long ago that is. It was only 21 years after the end of World War II. A couple of the priests were ex-servicemen. They stood out as sober serious types, some of the younger priests being markedly less certain in temperament.

At the start of 1966, Australia's currency was still pounds, shillings and pence. The priests dressed like Catholic priests had for centuries – black soutanes to their ankles and white clerical collars. The White Australia policy was very recent history, colour TV had yet to be imported. It was before the summer of love and Woodstock, before student revolts and sexual liberation and the women's movement. It was a more silent world, more introvert. People who were good with words were suspect: they were selling something – worst of all, an idea of themselves. That was called 'being on yourself'. You didn't want to be thought of as being on yourself at the old school; it made you a target.

The biggest excitement to sweep the school in my first year was when kids 'pissed off'. Escaped *Shawshank Redemption* style, stuffing their beds with towels and putting footballs on the pillow to fool the dormitory masters who did night patrols with a torch. The year before I arrived, a kid called Brushy Matthews was said to have got as far as Surfers Paradise in Queensland. It was further said that the night before he escaped the island, Brushy burnt his blue school blazer with the sacred letters 'AM' on its crest. That was wild!

(I'm driving my three-year-old grandson to day care, he doesn't want to go. We're rounding a corner when he works one hand free, opens the car door and says, 'I not going,' and tries to jump. Fortunately, his seatbelt restrains him. 'He did a Brushy Matthews,' I tell Tim.)

Other escapees got as far as Launceston and Hobart; a couple hid out for some days in the bush. All were duly recaptured, returned, and flogged to make them submissive, but no matter how brutal the authorities were in enforcing their many rules and regulations, there were always kids prepared to take their chances. And that – to be frank – thrilled me. Like the night two outlaws had a competition to see who could go to confession the most times during evening chapel. I don't know what the final score was, but I do recall the priest, our gentle ineffectual music master, bursting from his side of the confessional and ordering them to *confess no more*!

In my third year, a group of kids arrived from Hobart. For different reasons, including expulsion, they had all left the big Catholic school for boys in Hobart. They were mostly older and had attitude. Within weeks, the Hobart gang had bought a Simca Aronde, a quaint little French car best described by the fact that the word *aronde* translates as 'swallow' (the bird, not the gulp). They purchased it from a local caryard for the grand sum of $105, conning Brother Jim, who mowed the school lawns and was a bit simple, to sign the relevant papers.

At night, the Hobart gang would sneak out and go joy riding. That lasted until the priest I'm calling Eric discovered the vehicle and removed the rotor arm from the distributor. Eric was seriously scary. Most of us would have fled the crime scene at this point, but the kid who was the brains behind the operation led a night raid which stole the rotor arm out of the distributor of the only other Simca Aronde in town and got their car going again. Eric apprehended the gang shortly afterwards and the brains behind the operation was expelled, but the audacity of the crime sent a wave of excitement through the school, particularly the fact of getting Brother Jim to sign the papers. It felt like my first glimpse into organised crime.

My first glimpse of a capital offence came in my first year, when Smithie (not his real name) knocked off the tuck shop. Smithie was from a Bass Strait island and uninhibited in ways I'd never imagined. Other kids could put him up to doing strange things. One day I saw some kids dare him to hunt a dog that had strayed onto the junior oval. He stalked it and brought it crashing down, yelping and snapping.

At night, someone would put him up to swinging naked across the girders in the dormitory ceiling. The whisper would hurry from bed to bed, 'Smithie's off again!' You'd look up and see this pale shape, long cock flapping, lapping the dormitory ceiling like a gibbon in the zoo. If he fell, he could break a rib or a leg or both. If the dormitory master appeared and caught him in the beam of his torchlight, he'd be told to go to the priest's room at the end of the dormitory. We'd all lie in the dark and listen as the cane whipped through the air and bit his skin. Smithie would emerge squirming with pain and we'd lie there, hyperalert to the whole drama. No circus act was ever half as enthralling.

★

Other things to happen in my first year.

My first friend at the school was a kid I'll call Stuart. After we had come back from the first-term holidays, he said he had a story he wanted me to hear. We went and sat outside one of the classrooms in the empty bottom corridor. There, in the big eerie space that is a school without kids, he told me his mother had committed suicide. His mother had committed suicide and he'd been sent back to boarding school! Shortly thereafter, he started behaving differently towards me and the friendship vanished.

In my year was a kid I'll call Jagger, who, it was said, had been adopted from an orphanage. He was one of the pair who ran away and hid in the bush for a few days. Early, I saw Jagger fight. I like boxing, and think I have a reasonable eye for it as sport. Jagger fought like Mike Tyson. He dropped his head and charged his opponent, swinging a blizzard of overhead punches at his opponent's face. It was scary to behold as he could do serious damage quickly. Everyone was wary of him. You paid homage to Jagger's pride if you encountered him in a corridor or on the school property.

One day I saw Jagger bash a kid at the basketball court. The boy was a 'day kid' who was excessively confident for the old school, the sort who had been raised to express a view. I met him decades later. He was still hurt and indignant about what happened this day.

I need to be clear about a couple of things. Bashing is not boxing. In boxing, the fighters are matched by weight and ability. A boxer enters the ring knowing he or she will hit and be hit. A bashing is when one party is defenceless. Anyone who knows fighting understands when that is – boxing has strict rules governing it. Bashing has no rules. At boarding school, the victim might lift his fists in a gesture of self-defence, but that's part of what made bashings such wretched sights to behold. To retain any semblance of pride, the boy being bashed had to be seen to make some semblance of a fighting effort – this, in turn, vindicated the attack.

There's also a big difference between throwing a punch and flinging your fists about. Throwing a punch is like hitting a golf ball or hitting a cover drive with a cricket bat – there's a skill, an inherent ability, to it. Jagger could punch. He was sitting on the other kid who couldn't get his head away from the blows. The other kid eventually emerged from the grass rubbing his eyes and crying. I did nothing.

That could be one way of summarising the first three years of my boarding-school experience: I did nothing and I did nothing and I did nothing. What I now know is that if you do nothing often enough, you end up with a dead weight of nothing inside you.

They had initiations. I was 'dyked' – my head was shoved down a toilet while it was flushed. Didn't bother me. I'm not going to pretend things bother me that don't. Life's hard enough without bearing imaginary loads. I also now know that the kid who led my dyking was being serially abused by one of the priests at the time.

I was held down and had my nuts blacked with nugget. Didn't bother me. It was another initiation and I'd passed. What did bother me was a form of bullying I hadn't witnessed before, one where a kid was put in the middle of a circle and not let out. Twice I saw kids run around frothing and screaming, sheets of snot hanging from their noses. I did nothing.

One day they did it to a kid I'll call Charlie Durham. Charlie was physically awkward, bad acne, not academic, but a good kid. For the first time, I saw what it means to be alone in an amoral universe – totally alone, beyond any idea of hope or mercy. *My God, my God, why have you forsaken me?* Charlie stood self-consciously with his arms crossed. It was like he knew his lot in life was to be unloved. Lifting his pimple-scarred face, he looked his tormentors in the eye, trying to muster such dignity as the situation permitted. That moment haunts me to this day. *I wish to Christ I'd stood with you, Charlie!*

★

Do I wish I had been able to fight? I certainly would've liked the option. I once said as much to John Embling, a friend of mine who ran a shelter for street kids in the western suburbs of Melbourne for 30 years. Embling had experiences like a bikie gang turning up at his door demanding he hand over a kid who had dudded them on a drug deal. In addition to possessing a hyperactive intellect, Embling was a student of hand-to hand combat and knew all sorts of ways to kill and disable, which he taught to young women living on the streets. He said maybe I was lucky, that being skilled in violence just presents you with a whole new set of dilemmas. How do you do violence responsibly?

As it was, I didn't get into a fight during my school years. Embling's father, who was a commando during World War II, said the best form of self-defence is 'staying nondescript'. That's basically what I did, at least in the early years. What troubled me was being a mute witness to other kids' pain and humiliation. What I felt at such moments was best described by a friend, who had similar school experiences at an elite Melbourne private school, as 'a numb paralysis'. From the harsh chorus of voices that accompanied such moments, I also absorbed the idea that if you're a man, you fight. If you don't fight, you're a coward. I was also to meet this attitude plenty of times on the sports field. The only thing in my life I have ever really fought for is my journalism – fought, in the words of Jack Kerouac, with the energy of a benny addict. Like my life depended on it. Learning from each fight.

How do I rationalise writing on boxing? Easy. Boxing is consensual and highly regulated: violence is neither. Violence has a logic all its own, which most people understand innately and fear, since it points to a whole other human order. What overwhelmed me at 11 was seeing how, once violence enters the scene, every other human regard is either diminished or disappears. I desperately wanted to make it stop, but I didn't. If I say that to people now, they say – but you couldn't, you were only a boy. True, but that knowledge doesn't change the impact it had on my being. From the start, my inaction in the face of violence seemed a colossal moral failure. I felt deep shame, the sort that corrupts and corrodes.

In Year 11, I discovered World War I poet Wilfred Owen. His poems were panoramic in their scope and detail, and played like movies before my eyes. In 'Strange Meeting', he describes a dream he has of hand-to-hand battle in the enemy trenches which he wins, presumably by stabbing his opponent to death with a bayonet. Then he sees the face of the dying German soldier and recognises it as his own – in killing another, he was killing part of himself. I got that.

At university, I studied the history of conscientious objection during World War I. I read about the abominable way conscientious objectors were treated. The image that lingers is of a man being strapped to the wheel of an artillery gun throughout a bombardment so that every massive explosion that accompanied the gun being fired tore through his brain while the cannon bucked and his body was wrenched about. I don't believe I could do that. It's the reason I'd never say I was a Christian. As I see the history of the world and the long list of powerful individuals who have killed (and worse) to protect their interests, to stand up for the truly powerless is to risk being crucified.

There was no Jesus in my world when I was 11. Maybe if there had been an adult around who had some insight into me, he or she might have said, 'You can get to people if you use the right words.' When I was nine I saved a girl with an intellectual disability being bullied. Walked between her and the bullies, took her arm and charmed our way out. But I was no longer a child. The paralysis of self-consciousness had set in. I needed a guide, a wise elder, but there wasn't one. Just a lot of kids making it up as we went along.

★

The three priests subsequently convicted of sex crimes were all in my orbit. I'll call them Tom, Roger and Greg – their true first names. Tom was small and lithe, neat in appearance and, unusually for a priest, tanned. He looked trim and taut like a rugby half-back. I must've met him with Mum and Dad before coming to the school because I had some preconception of him as a friendly, caring man. First day in class he was sharp and severe. Maybe he had to be that way – like a sergeant major with the new recruits – but his switch in persona shocked me.

Tom was sentenced to four years' imprisonment in 2019. One of the suggestions in the media subsequent to his conviction was that Tom had invited a boy to his room after the kid had confessed to him about having sexual urges in the confessional box – that is, confessed to him in his role as a priest. It would be a few more years before I graduated to masturbation and by then Tom had gone. Perhaps that saved me.

I once asked Tim what sort of a kid I was at that age. He said, 'Eager to please and a bit naïve.' One night two older boys suggested with grins on their faces that I should ask Tom for a 'sex lec'. Naively, I did.

Tom's 'sex lecs' have been much discussed in recent times in the media. His modus operandi was that he'd get kids to come to his room at night individually in their pyjamas, tell them about sex and then get the kid to pull out his cock. Tom would tap it or handle it to see if it was 'in working order'. According to the records of the court case, he got one of the two complainants to wank in front of him and, having done so, heard his confession. If you actually believed in the Catholic Church and the sanctity of its rituals, that would turn your psyche inside out. It also emerged at the trial that Tom had been sexually abused by a priest as a child.

I got in and out of Tom's room untouched – but I remember liking his discreet lighting, the tone of his voice purring like a gentle motor ... and, of course, I wonder why nothing happened to me. I was never more vulnerable than I was at that moment. Basically, I only knew about sex what he was telling me.

Roger, who was sentenced to four years' imprisonment in 2008, taught second year, so he was around but I didn't yet have him for a teacher. Tim told me not to trust him, said he had favourites. There was always one kid, invariably athletic, in Roger's company. To be fair, I met one of them after Roger was convicted and he was surprised by what Roger was alleged to have done. He said he'd seen none of it and I didn't disbelieve him.

Roger was feline in his movements and markedly reserved. He had eyes that could look sideways from behind big glasses and see things no-one else could. He and I were like a cat and a dog. I didn't think he liked me, but I didn't hold that against him. I was well on the way to not liking me.

Greg, the third priest from my time to go to jail, was around but his breakout year, when he went totally off the rails, would come in my sixth and final year. Greg was plump and aged about 30 and capable, in an impulsive way, of being kind and thoughtful. But one thing I knew about him almost from the start – he was immature. The kids laughed at him behind his back. He'd do something outrageous to get the kids onside one moment and then be stern the next because he'd lost control of the class and had to restore order. It was like he genuinely wanted to play with the kids and then he'd remember he was an authority figure and have to play that part – always, I felt, reluctantly.

★

There was plenty going on. In the refectory, we sat at tables of six. The school bully was at my table. We'll call him Chris. He was about 16, taller than most other kids, quick and effective with his fists, and had a permanent scowl on his face. I'm well aware if I met him now, I might like him. I remember meeting a kid I saw do a brutal act at boarding school years later. He was someone I didn't expect to like, but he was actually a gentle person and I felt within him a great sadness, a sadness we both recognised, to do with who and what we were in those years and the things we did to survive.

Nonetheless, I was the sole witness when Chris bashed Rinso. Rinso had arrived at the school late, starting in third year. I was intrigued by him. His real name was Paul McMahon and he had a gentlemanly manner like he'd stepped out of the Edwardian era. His mother had equipped him with an all-white outfit for physical education – white socks, sandshoes, shorts and t-shirt. That got him dragged through the mud and the name Rinso.

They came for Rinso, and he had six or seven fights in a row. But Rinso could actually fight. He knew how to punch and threw them straight which maximised his reach. His unusually independent path led inevitably to Chris. Chris hit Rinso before he got his fists up. Rinso responded gamely but he was much too small, and his punches didn't reach their target. Down the front of Rinso's white shirt was a big splash of red. I was 50 or 60 metres away at the other end of an empty corridor, watching in horrified silence.

So there I was at age 11 sitting at the same table as Chris. If I reached for the butter or jam, it would amuse him to hit me across the knuckles with his knife so that I was left with small serrated rows of blood blisters on my knuckles. Tim fronted him. Fifty-odd years later, I can't think of that moment without getting emotional. There is nothing more ugly than real violence – the recipient is exposed in the most pitiful, hopeless, humiliating way. Tim was younger and smaller than Chris and couldn't fight to save himself. I saw fear flush through his face but he stood squarely in front of the bully and said, 'You do that again to my brother and I'll go to the rector.' Chris looked perplexed, his brow knitted – then abruptly he turned and walked off.

That was as brave as I saw it get at boarding school. For me. My brother.

★

The rector was a big man, Germanic, with ice blue eyes and fine grey hair. I'll call him Herman. Most feared of all the priests, including by other priests. Tim saw Greg hide from him one day after Greg flounced out of class saying he wasn't being respected and the class became chaotic. Herman appeared, restored order, then went looking for Greg who darted into an enclave until Herman had passed.

I was told by big kids that Herman sliced so deep with the cane he could split a pillow. I believed it. He trod noiselessly. With his soutane coming to his ankles, he moved like a black chess piece carrying its own brand of silent terror.

One day Herman appeared from nowhere at the open door of our classroom. I didn't see him but I heard all noise evaporate. In the empty silence, I heard Herman call my name. He beckoned me to follow him. It was like everyone in the room gasped and, with that, came a sense of being deeply known in a way you don't want to be known. Known in all your sweaty private places. You weren't allowed to show fear but my hair was tingling with it. The floor swam beneath my feet. I had crossed into another world of sensation like you do on drugs.

Corporal punishment is ceremonial pain. Herman was into the ceremony of it. His wordlessness was frightening since it emphasised that his power was absolute. I followed his giant black back and immaculately clipped silver head, saw kids grin as we passed, enjoying the spectacle. I didn't know what offence I had committed.

At the door of his office, he indicated with a nod that I should wait outside. I had a burning sensation in my forehead like my middle eye was on fire. I tried to calm myself by looking at a faded Albert Namatjira print on the wall but the fear kept coming in waves like nausea. Herman reappeared, a giant in the doorframe. He beckoned and turned without even waiting to see if I obeyed his command, so confident was he of his power. Again I followed his great black back. When we got inside, I tried to speak in my defence, and he exploded like he was incensed at the intrusion, 'Before I cane you, Flanagan ...', he cried, and suddenly I was melting in a strange heat, begging him not to hit me.

He came round his desk and held me as tenderly as a woman might.

In 2019, Steve O'Halloran alleged Herman did something similar with him. But he said Herman put his hand on his thigh and inside his underpants. If my experience had a sexual dimension, I was unaware of it. The truth is Herman did calm me, but I left his room knowing I'd lost something I'd never get back. For the first and only time in my life, I'd begged for mercy, and there were two people in the world who knew it, me and Herman. That would be our weird secret.

It occurs to me now that Tim and I laughed about the old school for years before we actually talked about it. When we were both in our 60s, he told me that Herman had marched him to his office. Each week we were given work duties – picking up papers in the yard etc – and Herman accused him of not doing the one he had been assigned. But he had – Tim was a highly conscientious kid. He was also, in his own words, a bit self-righteous. He told Mum, Mum drove the 80 miles of bush roads from Rosebery and fronted Herman. This marked Tim as a kid who would carry stories back to his parents. I wouldn't have told my parents, but sooner or later I would have told my brother.

Curiously, Herman told Dad at some point that he thought I might have a vocation as a priest. This was received with great mirth in my family who regarded me as hopelessly irreligious.

Our dormitory master was a priest I'll call Biggles. He was about 40, mild in manner but odd in his behaviour – although, at the time, along with everything else, it seemed normal. Having been made an officer in the school cadet corps, Biggles had a spell in which he would emerge from his office/bedroom at the end of our dormitory each morning wearing his officer's cap. Under his arm would be one of those sticks that sergeant majors carry on the parade ground to measure the marching step of new recruits. We'd be lined up in three rows, military-style, Biggles would shout, 'Fingernails OUT!', and as one, 80 pairs of hands would jump out, stiffly held. With a couple of kids following him like adjutants, Biggles would march up and down the lines, inspecting fingernails.

Biggles gave me my first caning. He had two footprints chalked out on the red carpet in his room – I was told to stand on them and bend over. I was both scared and curious. It was the weirdest sensation, like an electric shock snaking around the cheeks of your arse. Afterwards it was strangely exciting, bum burning merrily like a log fire in winter. I was on the other side of the dorm showing kids my red cheeks and re-enacting Biggles' swing when he called out, 'Don't exaggerate, Flaps!', and a group of older boys laughed. Normally, the derision of older boys fell upon my ears like acid, but this time I hardly cared. I'd got the cuts and hadn't cried! I'd passed another test.

★

Best day of the year? House sports. Brilliant blue sky, sparkling Bass Strait, spiky lush green grass beneath my bare feet. I was runner-up Under 12 athletics champion, losing to Tony 'Humber' Maguire, brother of Paddy who did the Tarzan impersonation at the Northern Tasmanian Independent Schools Swimming Sports.

At the end of the year there was a big assembly and the athletics prizes were handed out. My prize for runner-up Under 12 athletics champion, a school pennant with your name inked upon it, went to a kid who wasn't even in our division. I shall never forget him skipping happily towards the podium to receive my prize, a look of surprised delight on his face. The fact he hadn't been in any of the events didn't seem problematic to him.

I complained to the priest in charge of the sports awards, a former truck driver who was a bit thick. 'Well, that's the way the results came to me, Flanagan,' he said, terminating the conversation by walking off.

That year a craze swept the school for peroxided hair. Kids appeared with yellow-blond mops while others went orange. Herman addressed a school assembly, saying, 'It has come to my notice that there are boys in this school who wish to make themselves look more stupid than the Good Lord, in his wisdom, intended them.' The Beatles had broken internationally and with them had come something else Herman didn't like – mop-top hairdos. That year as every kid stepped up to be photographed for the school magazine they were checked by Herman to see if they had a fringe. For those deemed to have one, a stick embedded in a can of axle grease awaited – Tim can even remember the brand, Ampol. I didn't have a mop-top but I did have a fringe. A swipe with the stick and it was fixed to the top of my head like a galah's crest. I remember washing the axle grease out of my hair that night – it was thick and dirty yellow and had a grainy essence.

That's a rough summary of my first year. I was 11. I didn't think to tell any of it to my parents. It was beyond language and would remain that way until my mid-20s, when my wife was preparing to have our first child.

★

When I arrived for my first year there was a fantastic newness to everything – it felt like being on a film set, new characters stepping out from behind every door. By the second year, the freshness had gone and in its place was a mind-numbing routine. At night in a dormitory of 80 kids, there was always someone snoring or talking, which kept me awake. I became neurotic about noise and remain so. I struggled to stay awake in class and acquired a reputation for laziness.

We spent hours in chapel, trailing in and out every

THE EMPTY HONOUR BOARD

day. We woke each morning to a clap of the dormitory master's hands, slid out of bed, knelt and prayed. We went to bed with prayers, started every lesson and meal with them. A river of pious language wound through our days like a river of dead fish. I developed the art of not listening. We were rostered to serve as altar boys. One kid I served with as an altar boy took regular swigs of altar wine when the priest wasn't looking, the same act that allegedly triggered George Pell into a sexual frenzy three decades later. I had a swig or two myself.

Each night, we had two sessions of evening study amounting to two hours for juniors and two-and-a-half hours for seniors. No-one spoke and only in the last 20 minutes of the second session were we allowed to read a book of our own choice. Priests patrolling study marched through the rooms with their missals held in front of their faces, like orienteers reading maps telling them which way to go spiritually.

We saw the end of the evening news after evening chapel. The television was up in a corner of the school library. One TV, over 150 kids. It had a magnifying screen which made the figures larger when viewed front-on and distorted when viewed from the side. Some Saturday nights we had films – Doris Day/Rock Hudson sorts of movies – safe, inane, 1950s Americana. There was no music in the dormitories. Some kids had transistors, most didn't.

In this grey world, I discovered sport. Discovered

it like a prospector discovers gold after years in the wilderness. Sport, unlike school and religion, had *life*! I discovered sport like others I have read discover theatre – as a magical space where aspects of humanity otherwise kept hidden away come out to play. For the first time, I saw grace. I'd heard plenty about grace as a religious quality without having any idea of what was being talked about. Now I saw athletic grace that took my breath away, acts of skill and daring that imprinted themselves indelibly upon my brain. It was like having visions and here's the first – a blue flash cutting sideways through a pack, gathering the ball in transit and goaling on his left foot. That's Rodney Oborne, later to play with Collingwood and Richmond, when he was a 12-year-old.

The sports field was dramatic. It was intensely comic. You saw inside people, saw their private pretensions and conceits. It was violent. In my very first game in the Under 13Bs, we were playing the town's tough new high school. My opponent met me with the words, 'If you get the ball, I'm going to punch you in the face.' I was deeply shocked but, even so, wasn't tempted to leave the field. I loved being out there. All my senses came zooming to life. It was the closest thing to a drug trip I had before I had a drug trip. What sort of a footballer was I? Timid but fascinated.

★

The mythologies I'd inherited at birth were British Imperial and Irish Catholic/Irish convict (Tim told me early on that 'we' didn't stand for 'God Save the Queen'). Now I found a mythology that was immediate and obvious. This was the year Wynyard played North Hobart for the state premiership at Burnie's West Park oval. North Hobart full forward Dicky Collins was kicking for goal after the siren to win the match when the Wynyard fans, a notoriously excitable lot, claimed Collins had marked the ball after the siren, and pulled out the goalposts so he couldn't take his shot. I was there. The umpire, whose name was Pilgrim, never blew his whistle to signal the end of the game. It's still being played in the footy dreamtime …

Cricket was the summer sport. I'm old enough to remember when you got to know Test cricket through the medium of radio. Tim and I played countless Test matches in the backyard. I didn't wear shoes from the start of the summer holiday to the end. After the holiday, back at school, feet cramped and sweaty in shoes, I was bored again.

I set my mind to making time go faster. An Under 14 cricket match I was interested in was being played on successive Saturday mornings. It occurred to me that perhaps if I concentrated sufficiently hard on hurrying time along, I could make the school week go faster. Sort of like blowing on a candle to make the flame bend. For a week I sat with my eyes clenched, and when I unclenched them Robert Bird, a terrific young sportsman who played football for Tasmania at the age of 19, was opening the bowling for Burnie High School. Good line and length from the first ball, game immediately alive in my head and, yes, there was a sense in which the last seven days hadn't happened. I thought about doing it again but it took too much concentration.

Tim and I were in the school band. I was third cornet, he was solo tenor horn. Neither of us had much idea. I was like one of those cyclists in the Tour de France who drop off the back of the peloton when they hit the hills, the hills being the high notes. I'd return near the end for the sprint to the line. We'd been pushed into the band because Mum wanted music in the family. Her grandparents' place had been full of music when she was a kid and, to her, it was a thing of communal joy. For me, if not for others, the band was a further weight of tedium.

At practice on Sunday morning, if we didn't play a number well enough, the pedantic priest running the show would make us play it again. The siren to end the first spell of morning study would have gone and you knew you were now in free time – and you only had 40 minutes of free time. I was once asked if I hated being at boarding school. I hated being kept in for band practice. Every five minutes it took you to play 'Edelweiss' (surely the most boring dirge ever written) was five minutes less *free* time you had before you were back in study, back in enforced silence, willing the time to pass. I wanted to be outside with the kids kicking the footy, playing end to end. I could watch them for hours like other people watch ocean waves forming and breaking.

Some kids were really good marks, could judge the flight of the ball and hold their line in the mass airborne collision that is a pack of bodies coming together. The best mark I saw was by a kid called Chris Bartlett. He came from the side – that is, perpendicular to the oncoming wall of players – held his position in the air when they smacked into him and took the ball with a single grab. This is the marking style made famous by Richmond champion Royce Hart – before then, no-one had either thought of it or was good enough to do it. I can still remember what Chris Bartlett was wearing – a sky-blue woollen jumper and jeans of a different style to everyone else's, but faded in the right places. I still recall the look on his face. He'd had the idea of marking from the side, and he did what he'd imagined.

I asked Herman if I could get out of the band. He replied with one word, 'No'. The band was as big a deal as the school possessed. We had different uniforms to the other boys, our coats were light blue, our trousers grey, we wore white shirts and ties. Twice in my time we competed interstate. The drum major had a big shouty voice. Unfortunately, I'd stopped listening to most of what was said to me.

One day, when the drum major, who stood in front of the band facing away from us, ordered us to turn right, I turned left. When he cried, 'Queeeeek march!', I queeeeek marched off in the wrong direction, the file of kids behind me following my lead, all of us merrily playing along on our instruments. At some point we knew we had lost contact with the rest of the band but we were having too much fun to stop. On we marched, playing 'Invercargill' or whatever the marching tune was, down the hill, out the gates and, ever so briefly, to freedom. Tim was in the band that day – it's his favourite story about me at boarding school. My 'One Flew over the Cuckoo's Nest' moment.

★

I only recall one of the teachers rousing me intellectually in my second year, an older priest we called Booze. He was ex-Navy, and would willingly slice your arse with a cane. He had a witch's nose, long and crooked with a lump on the end, a deep resonant voice and a somewhat theatrical manner. He was a hard man but as I judge such matters, he could teach. The course was called social studies, which meant he could, and did, talk about virtually anything. He interested me in American politics and, by questioning a shallow view I expressed on migrants, made me think seriously about the issue for the first time.

That year, on my report card under teacher's comments, Booze wrote: 'Martin is too emotional.' That puzzled me. What did 'too emotional' mean? I'd never shown visible emotion in front of him. One morning I reported sick at the infirmary. The priest running the infirmary that day – I'm not sure, might have been Roger – insinuated I was putting it on. Maybe he was right. This sort of thing put the idea in my head, never to totally depart, that I was emotionally inauthentic.

In that second year, I had Roger for a couple of subjects. He had little gift for teaching, having minimal presence and delivering information in a mumbling monotone, but he did save my arse one day when he intercepted a note I'd sent across the room with unkind words about another boy. He just said, 'I don't think you'd want [the boy's name] to read this, would you?', and scrunched it up.

When Roger's court case came up, I knew one of his accusers. I remembered seeing him one night in a quiet rage, his older brother trying to reason with him and calm him down. It was obvious the older brother was uncomfortable about their conversation being heard, but what they were talking about I have no idea. At the end of a long process involving several retrials, Roger was found guilty of 'touching' three boys in his room and having them 'touch' him. He was sentenced to prison where he continued to deny his guilt.

That year, I had the only woman teacher in the

school, for English. She was as gentle as a flower and, under the circumstances, remarkably brave. Thank you, Liz Hamilton. When a tough boy in the year above me made a crude remark about you, I was offended on your behalf but didn't know what to say.

★

Otherwise the routine of my days was tediously male – pre-pubescent boys, adolescents, hairy young men, priests. As in prison, it was a case of doing time. The boys who provided the entertainment were the naughty ones who risked getting caught and did get caught and were punished on a regular basis. It was as if they made some inner deal with pain and didn't let it stop them being who they were. They fascinated me but I was never one of them.

I think that's why a kid I'll call Marconi loathes me, or did the night I saw him in a restaurant a decade or so after leaving school. He was with a group of work-mates, loudly controlling the conversation as he had in the classroom, when he saw me and shouted across the restaurant, 'There he is – Flanagan the coward!' But there was good reason to be fearful. There were kids like Jagger around. You wouldn't want to get caught looking at him the wrong way. As for the priests, they were all scary in their own unique way, but the three who could make the air freeze were Booze, Herman and Eric.

I'm calling him Eric after Eric Burdon and the Animals, Eric Burdon being hairy, our Eric being largely bald. He had a big chest and sucked air between his teeth and went red in the face with barely suppressed anger. Before I got to the school, Eric was sent to New Zealand for some reason. When he returned, he performed a haka for a few of the kids, Tim among them. The haka would have suited him perfectly, the fierce compression erupting in a shout from the pit of his being. He had that sort of energy in him.

Eric had an impossible workload, doing most of the physical work around the school, like laying concrete for the new science block, while also fulfilling senior academic roles like master of studies. Eric took wrongdoing by the kids personally. He punched one kid and, to my knowledge, threatened to punch at least two others.

Eric was terrifying, and no-one dared cause him offence, which is why Tim made me laugh when I was outside the courtroom waiting to give evidence against Greg. We were sitting on a wooden bench holding takeaway coffees. For a time Eric made a big milk can of cocoa each night for the kids. We filed past him in silence, plastic cups outstretched, as he ladled away. I can still taste it – thin and watery and sweet. The kids called it 'choko'. *Remember the night the kids found one of Eric's bandaids in the choko?* A whole group of kids electrified by a dangerous secret. Had Eric got wind of the joke (while undertaking yet another labour on our behalf!), he would have had a thermonuclear implosion.

But no matter how scary the priests might be, there was always a subversive voice in the place that was never subdued or eliminated. Herman physically terrified me, but he didn't spiritually terrify me – he didn't conjure up visions of Hell and scare me with the idea I was going there. There were only a handful of kids among the boarders of my time who appeared to take the religion of the school seriously. One was Tim. Another was a quiet, deeply conservative kid from a farming family. I saw him get bashed in my first year – I can still see his head banging against the brick wall behind him with the force of the blow.

The Academy Award for the most frightening priest in those early years goes to Herman. I think of him as a performance artist whose art was fear. When his movie-star profile, silver hair, cold blue eyes appeared at a window, something inside every kid rolled up like an armadillo and you prayed it was someone else's name you heard uttered in his low resonant silvery voice.

Tim was in a class once when a truck pulled up outside and Herman said, 'Don't anyone look out the window.' Paul O'Halloran, then aged 14, took a glance. Herman gave him four cuts for it. I can imagine the ceremony – the hurt, the humiliation, the sense of injustice in his heart burning like the cheeks of his arse.

I did an interview once with Irish comedian Dave Allen. We talked about the fearful nature of silence in

Catholic schools of our generation. He told me about being chucked out of a class and ordered to sit in the corridor. His sole concern was not being spotted by the school's equivalent of Herman. Telling the story, he impersonated a kid, head hunched down, trying to reduce himself to a visible nothing as the Herman figure approaches. He made the licking sound of his rubber soles on the linoleum floor. That was the story: no words, just the licking sound getting closer and closer …

★

I always liken the part played by the priests in our school to the role of American helicopter gunships during the Vietnam war. The gunships only controlled Vietnamese villages while they buzzed in the air above them, guns protruding from every portal. Once the choppers tilted and flew away, the guerrillas came out of the jungle and resumed control. Once the priest left the classroom during the day or the dormitory at night, kids like Marconi took over. He wasn't the funniest kid, but he was the loudest and he never stopped. Certainly, the priests never stopped him. He was brave, if that's the word. There were just things he didn't seem to feel.

Years later, I met someone who knew Marconi's family and told me his father used to dominate whole rooms, and then, when he had everyone's attention, belittle his son. That's what Marconi did – turn his tongue on a kid and get others to join in. (Thinking back to Marconi and his use of nicknames, I am reminded of another boarding-school graduate, Donald Trump, and his use of nicknames – I would love to read a book on Trump's schooldays!)

Mostly, I think Marconi was motivated by a desperate desire for centre stage, but what he did could cross into bullying and I'm not sure he knew the difference. One afternoon I saw him leave a boy sobbing after a shrill week-long campaign from Marconi's tongue finally stripped the kid of his last vestige of pride. I had that boy in mind many years later when I wrote the line: 'I saw kids broken at my school and I wonder if they ever mended.' Maybe Marconi noticed that I said nothing and despised me on moral grounds. Or maybe he grew contemptuous of me because I watched the entertainment provided by naughty kids like him without ever providing entertainment of my own.

I only heard of one kid who evaded the cane for any length of time. He was a small, devout day boy with a Germanic name. They got him in the end for a crumpled-up piece of paper under his desk, or that was the story. Waiting for the cane was worse than getting the cane. One rare weekend, Mum and Dad had business which caused them to drive up from the West Coast. They took me out for an afternoon. That morning, I was caught in the dormitory a few minutes after we were allowed to be there. Biggles called out my name and said, as they customarily did, 'Come and see me tonight.'

I could make a film about that day of the quiet moody sort the Scandinavians made in the 1960s and '70s. About a 12-year-old kid realising his parents are of secondary importance in the central drama of his life. It was like I was a specimen in a glass jar and they were figures moving around outside it.

Come night, in your pyjamas, you waited in a queue outside the discipline master's office to be caned. Everyone wanted to go first. Get in, get it over with. In my third or fourth year, half a dozen kids snuck out for a night on the town and got caught coming back. The following day – a Saturday – was hot. Eric had the escapees labouring on a series of tasks, at one point buying each a bottle of fizzy cordial to quench their hard-earned thirst. How strange must it have been for Eric, being kind to these kids in the afternoon when, come that night, he was going to hurt them and not in a trivial way. And, so, the odd mood of the day inten-sified until, come night, we watched from our beds as the door of Eric's office at the end of the dormitory opened, a chunk of yellow light fell out, and each kid was beckoned in. Eric was in earnest that night, laying them on, and there's the last kid in the line, the last of the six, hearing the swish of the cane through the air, registering each stroke as it licked the skin before cutting it apart, and he's dancing about, pacing from side to side and rubbing his arse, because he knows what's coming and he can't get away, like a fish writhing about on a hook.

All 150 boarders showered together in open showers. Nudity was law. That meant everyone saw the stripes across the arse of the kids who'd been caned. Initially you were left with a white welt studded with blood blisters, hot red flesh on either side. That was followed within a day by thin vivid bruises – greys and purples and reds – which thickened into softer grey clouds and turned brown before disappearing. You could measure time by the marks on other boys' arses. One week, two weeks, three weeks, a month …

Eric told me once that Tommy Button (made-up name) and I bruised the worst of any kids in the school. Tommy Button was this pale little kid with an oversize head and an ultra-polite manner. He had two big things going against him. One is that he was what was then called a 'Pom'. And, of the 150-odd boarders, he was one of only two who were uncircumcised. As I say to Tim, imagine how Tommy Button felt.

That was also the year a kid told me he'd 'rooted' his sister. He certainly didn't win her with his looks – he was a skinny, ugly youth. I wasn't entirely clear about sex but I did have two sisters. I echoed what he had said, clearly with a confused look on my face: 'You had sex with your sister?' Realising he had made a different impression to the one he anticipated, he said hurriedly, 'You don't have to go on about it! Everyone does it.'

It was also towards the end of that year when I overheard a conversation down the back of the classroom, a couple of kids talking and laughing about a priest I'll call Groucho, how he used to get kids in his room and wrestle with them on his bed and when he got up he'd have a bone in his trousers. Groucho got excited by rough play.

That was the first time I ever heard anything about sexual behaviour between priests and boys. About the same time Tim overheard a similar conversation about Groucho. By this time, I'd had my 'sex lec' from Tom and got out of his room unmolested. Tim had a sex lec from Tom and also emerged unmolested. Greg, from what I know, was merely being an immature git – e.g. doing a science experiment with potassium and water, putting a bit of extra potassium in to jazz up the experiment and blasting off his eyebrows.

It was either this year or the next that Tim saved me from one of Greg's moments of excess. Greg sent me up for something trivial like yawning in class and, when I questioned him, he told me to ask for extra punishment for challenging his authority. The extra punishment meant four cuts. I'd never had four. The most I'd had were two – you'd have to stay bending over and wait another two times for the stinging pain. Scared, I told Tim. He took Greg on. I stood outside Greg's door in the priests' quarters and listened. Greg shouted at Tim, Tim shouted at Greg. I was called in. Greg looked bewildered and defeated. Case dismissed.

Tim's intervention on that occasion may have protected me down the path. Greg never made a move on me but I do recall entering his room one night in my third or fourth year. He was performing like Bugs Bunny, babbling on for an audience of four or so kids in pyjamas sitting on his bed. He had an old-fashioned machine in his room for losing weight. You strapped a length of canvas around your arse and got jiggled. Greg had a big rear and was trying to reduce its dimensions.

He stood on the machine and danced, making a wanking motion with his right hand as he did, saying to his audience on the bed, 'Flanagan doesn't know what I mean.' I had yet to discover wanking and left his room in that in-between state where you're not entirely sure what you've just witnessed – but I didn't dwell on the matter. It promptly joined the pile of things left lying like dirty washing on the floor of my mind.

At the end of my second year, Jagger, the kid I feared most, lost a fight in a way that was both amazing to watch and highly instructive. As I wrote previously, his fighting method was to drop his head, protect his face and charge his opponent, blindly throwing a whirlwind of punches. Jagger rushed a thin sinewy kid from a mining town on the West Coast called Peter Newport, who coolly stepped aside and caught Jagger on the way through with an uppercut, flush in the face. It was over. Jagger was one preposterous bluff. He was as scared as the rest of us and after the holidays he didn't return.

So that was second year. It was a rough place but I was handling it. I had some dim idea that I might be doing so at a price, but basically I was going okay. The next year, my third, was the big one.

★

Come back in time to 1968, back to concrete open showers, lots of steaming flesh, everyone on total display. Tommy Button may have had to cope with the oddity of having an uncircumcised cock but I'm a clear year younger than any other kid in my class – some of them are more than two years older. They're all getting hair on their balls and I'm not. The man/boy thing has come into play. Some kids in the classroom have girl-friends. One has two. I suffer the humiliation of losing my last baby tooth and am left with a tell-tale gap in my gum, which the school photographer highlights in his garishly over-colourised portrait. I hide the picture deep in my school desk.

The rest of my class are in the school cadet corps, but the minimum age for the cadets is 14. I'm the only kid in third year who's still playing football in the Under 13s. As captain of the team and in the absence of any supervising adult, I assume the role of coach, which somehow comes naturally. But it means I'm playing with 'the littlies', as William Golding calls them in *Lord of the Flies*. This is the year adolescence hits like a tsunami.

I want to make it clear that the day boys had virtually no part in the narrative I'm now outlining. The day boys, otherwise known as 'day rats', were from another planet. You could like day boys, and have relationships with them, but there was a level of psychodrama to the place which they couldn't know. They came and went – you stayed. They arrived in the morning, hopefully with plenty of food, and left in the afternoon, lunchboxes empty. Scrounging food (called 'scunging') was a hard-practised, competitive art. Eric hated it. He said the food provided by the school was 'perfectly adequate'. Imagine, if you can, a stew with gravy that looked like grey clag, containing a few cubes of gristle served with a blob of powdered mash potato. Most kids got by on bread and jam.

It would be wrong of me to convey the impression that all the kids in the boarding school were involved in bullying. They weren't, not by a long way. But what I only saw a couple of times was someone stand up for a kid being bullied. I saw one boy do it twice. He was someone no-one, myself included, much liked. He slapped my face one night in the dormitory over a minor disagreement. But twice I saw him step in and make the bullying of another kid his personal business.

He wasn't likable, but something I later observed as a journalist with a couple of political dissidents I met is that it's a great mistake to think that individuals who perform gutsy significant acts are necessarily likable. Maybe what makes them unlikable is also what makes them dissidents.

What I did see at boarding school was that lots of the kids either didn't know what was going on around them or didn't want to know. I'm not being judgemental – as adults, we turn a blind eye to abhorrent happenings in the world every day. But around now I became aware I was noticing things that no-one else seemed concerned about. I became aware of boys being broken. Left blubbering and alone. *My God, my God, why have you forsaken me?*

Who were 'they' who did the breaking? Maybe only two or three but at vital moments they always seemed to have helpers. A boy would be singled out for some fault or quality. The art lay in making the insult hurt, then working the wound. One night, as faceless voices taunted him from the dark, I watched tears ran down the face of the kid in the next bed. He was a simple country boy. Years later, I saw him serving petrol in a service station in Hobart and was too ashamed to say hello.

Another kid whose crime was that he had a 'wog' name came back from the showers to find his underpants hung on the end of his bed, shit stains out for the world to see. I was terrified – crippling humiliation was now part of the game.

Around this time I stood guard for a kid from a lower grade who stole two girlie magazines from a local newsagent. We were encouraged to carry holy medals with the image of Mary, the Mother of God, on them. I carried a picture of a smiling young woman kneeling bare-breasted at a beach.

Adolescent politics are fascist politics. I offended a powerful boy – by definition, one who had followers. I was alleged to have said a particular day boy could beat him in a fight. Did I? I have no memory of having done so, but I might have. Fights were a topic of conversation. In fairness to the powerful kid, such a view, if expressed, did put him in a degree of danger because it could be used to spark a confrontation.

When I twice tried to speak to the powerful boy and he pointedly ignored me, I knew I was in trouble. Suddenly, I had a new nickname, one which apparently had some connection to me being a teller of stories. To use a British boarding-school expression, I was sent to Coventry. A fear like a sort of radiation illness infiltrated my being. I went to bed with it, woke to it, lived with it every moment of the day. There was no bottom to the pain. I prayed to the God I'd been taught to believe in, Our Father Who Art In Heaven. There was nothing there. *My God, my God …*

I came into evening study to find the whole room

decorated with the name I'd been given. All over the walls, on my desk. When I sat down and opened my desk, cheeks burning, I found the name written inside my books. They'd found the over-coloured photo of me by the professional photographer and put it up above the blackboard for everyone to see. I looked pink and pathetic, a pretend adolescent.

They kill people in some cultures by turning their psychic forces against them. I tried to tell my brother Tim but couldn't explain. What was happening? Nothing was happening. What could Tim do? It was around now, for the first and only time, that I cried when I got the cane. The priest, Eric, said it was going to hurt him more than it hurt me and I believed him. He didn't want to hurt me and I didn't want to be hurt but that's where we found ourselves, Eric and I, trapped in a universe of hurt.

I don't know how long it went on, but when I was finally let out of my invisible cage, I was desperate to please. Before this, while I'd never stood up to bullies, I'd never been one. Now, for maybe 10 minutes, maybe less, I crossed to the other side. I didn't perform the act, it wasn't my idea. But in every act of bullying performed for a crowd, there is a Greek chorus who cheer the principal actor on, saying, 'Do it! Do it!', and I joined that chorus. Not for long but long enough, and the awful deed was done.

That year, two girls from our sister school were in

certain of our classes. A kid who could be dared to do anything dropped a scrunched-up piece of paper beneath one of them, tapped her shoulder, pointed and said, 'You've dropped your rags.'

I saw her collapse. Saw her try and hide her sobbing red face beneath her arm. I knew then you can hurt people so badly they hurt forever and that hurt can carry through generations, and in that way you damage the universe.

That's when Ralph's black weight burst upon my brain.

★

God didn't save me. Footy did. East Devonport came from nowhere to win the 1968 North West Football Union premiership.

East's captain-coach, Graeme 'Gypsy' Lee, had olive skin and oiled black hair parted neatly down one side. He wore number one because he was number one. Not everyone could kick drop kicks off their preferred foot – he could kick them off either foot. He skimmed through the centre of the ground punching long low passes, splitting defences.

Two years earlier, at the national carnival, Gypsy had captained Tasmania and come third in the award for the best player in Australia. I didn't know it then but Gypsy was also the first footballer of Tasmanian Aboriginal descent to play in the VFL/AFL, having been with St Kilda in the early '60s and returning to Tasmania after only three years because he promised his young wife he would.

East were like the competition's extras. In the previous six years, they had finished last five times and second last on the other occasion. They had a quaint jumper like none I'd ever seen – strawberry red with a big blob of white on top, and socks to match. The two local teams called themselves Tigers and Bulldogs, and prided themselves on the size of their snarls. I didn't like either of them.

Each Saturday afternoon we were let out to watch the local men's footy, but I wasn't into it before Gypsy came along. It lacked the athletic grace of schoolboy footy – it was heavy and obvious, relied on muscle, and came with lots of harsh unfriendly voices.

Gypsy played with dash and encouraged it in his players. They stood out as individual characters and, in that way, I got to know them. Part of the theatre of local footy in those days was that supporters crowded around their teams during the half-time and three-quarter-time huddles to hear the bush oratory of the coaches. I squeezed into East Devonport's huddle and heard Gypsy speak to his players. He didn't shout, he didn't rant. He didn't do fire and brimstone speeches like other coaches of that era. He spoke to his players – to what was inside them. He spoke to what was inside me. He told his players a fantastic story, about many being one, and I swear, on grand final day 1968, I saw a giant swan made up of 18 human parts take off and fly. It was the most creative act I'd ever seen.

What Gypsy and East Devonport did still keeps coming back to me, fresh as a Beatles song.

★

That same year, we were let out for a party. My first. That night was a series of firsts. One was hearing the Beatles' *Sergeant Pepper* album. The song that got me was 'With a Little Help from My Friends'. A day kid turned up at the party half-drunk and when Ringo sang, 'Lend me your ears,' he shouted, 'And I'll piss in it.'

I was sitting quietly in a corner beside a plump, pretty 15-year-old. A young woman. The word was she had 'a 19-year-old boyfriend with a car'. I was a 13-year-old without a bicycle. We talked a while and then I shyly slipped an arm around her and she didn't throw it off. I think I may have amused her in some way. At some point, our faces leaned together and she kissed me – expertly. I can still remember her tongue entering my mouth, its naked suggestion delivered ever so lightly. We live only to discover beauty, wrote Kahlil Gibran, all else is a form of waiting. My waiting had ended.

About six months later we were let out to a second party, this one on a farm. I nicked out with another girl/woman a couple of years older than myself and we ended up lying together in the top of a barn, a brilliantly cold moonlit night, her breast an ecstasy of warmth, feeling wholly alive to every dazzling thing in the world. I mean it when I say the feeling was divine, or as much of divinity as I knew.

The morning after I lay in the barn and held the young woman's breast, I took a big risk. It was the start of the school holidays and I hitchhiked the 350 kilometres home – Mum and Dad were now living in Hobart with my two younger siblings at the other end of the island. Hitchhiking wasn't as big a drama as pissing off, but it was a serious offence, because the school was legally responsible for your safety until you got home. You could get six for hitchhiking. You were required to travel on public transport in uniform, but the brave boys hid their uniforms, put out their thumbs and hoped the car that pulled over wasn't being driven by a priest. Normally I would have been too scared but the enchantment of the previous night was upon me.

Freezing starlit night had become glorious sunstruck day. I saw colours more brilliantly than I'd ever seen them. Cars stopped, I got in. All I had to do was sit and listen. People told me things, private things, things they couldn't tell other people. They could tell me because I was a kid and they were never going to see me again. Each time I got out of the car I was richer by a story and I knew at once that stories were the wealth I coveted.

My last lift was with a God-botherer who tried to convert me. He went hard, circling the subject like a sheepdog trying to push a sheep through a gate. But in the place where formal religion might have sat was the goddess in the barn; I could still feel her prodigious nudity and our perfect harmony with the night and every living thing within it. I'll never forget the God-botherer's last words to me: 'This may be the last time God ever speaks to you.'

By the time he dropped me off on the outskirts of Hobart, my life had changed. I'd discovered the promise of the road: to quote Jack Kerouac, 'Nothing behind me, everything ahead of me.' I'd discovered a source of stories as fascinating as any library. I had well and truly discovered the power of the opposite sex. I could end the whole story of my boarding-school life here, on this day. I'd escaped the place as a prison of the mind. Never again would I be captured by a group. And there were things I wasn't going to bother arguing about with my family anymore, like religion, because, to my mind, they were beyond argument. I was on my way.

★

Tim left at the end of that year, his fifth. In one way, school was harder on him than me. I compromised, he didn't. That's why he stood up to the school bully. That's why he took on Greg. He had applied himself zealously to both his religion and his studies and then, in his fifth year, he'd been made a prefect. He was too serious-minded to be popular. Being a prefect also meant he had authority over older kids in the class above him. It all got too much and at the end of the year he left and went to Hobart High School.

When Mum and Dad asked me how I was getting on, I said okay because by now I was. If I'd arrived in fourth year my experience of the school would have been totally different. Each of my first three years was worse than the last. Each of my last three years was better than the one before – in my two final years, I only recall seeing one fight. In my fourth year, a new boy arrived, the son of English parents who had lived in various places around the world, including Africa. Quietly independent, he introduced me to a whole range of new interests like photography, Leeds United, the Kinks, the operettas of Gilbert and Sullivan, doing laboratory experiments for fun. We were both early appreciators of a convivial drink and became good friends. Thanks, Mike Sheppard – as much as any teacher, you broadened my view of the world.

Also in my fourth year, now being 14, I went to army camp as a cadet in the band. On the first night we lined up naked beneath our great coats and a doctor gripped our nuts and told us to cough. Didn't bother me but, from what I have read in the media, it did bother others. Kids from the other schools complained about the food. We went back for seconds.

I now read *Lord of the Flies* under the instruction of the one teacher who ever took me to any academic height, Father Bernard Hosie. He was no-nonsense, as befitting a man who'd flown in bombers during World War II, but he had a cultivated mind. Not all the kids liked him but he and I got on to the extent that I listened to what he said. I had him for English in fourth and fifth years and Modern History in my final year. I topped each of his classes and, for the first time in my life, thought I might be good at something.

On speech night in my fifth year, the senior English prize, which I had won, was awarded to another kid. I went to see Booze who had supervised prizes that year. He said, 'You got the oratory prize, Flanagan. One's enough.'

To be frank, I didn't really care. What did I care about? I cared whether the girl from Launceston I met at the school ball would reply to the letter I had written her. Not that she was the first young woman I had written to. The first was an extrovert with lots of sparkle – I was smitten. I sent her what I thought was a clever parody of William Blake's poem 'The Tyger'. She was unimpressed, merely replying that it had 'a couple of good lines'. I continued undaunted.

The highlight of my day was each evening, when Eric handed out the mail. A letter from a young woman could sustain me for days. First night I didn't even read it. I carried it like an egg. Then I'd allow myself a glimpse of the first page. Then a day or so later I'd read the rest and a reply would begin forming in my mind. That written and sent, the nervous wait for a reply would start anew.

I cared about sport – I've always said I learnt everything I know about sport by the time I was 16. And just as I had enjoyed doing English with Hosie in fourth and fifth year, I now enjoyed doing Modern History – which actually meant Modern British History – with him. It's where I acquired my lifelong interest in the Georgian era, from which Van Diemen's Land/Tasmania emerges, from which place I emerge.

What was more, I got an optimistic idea of history from studying the surge of events that led to the Great Reform Bill of 1832, which, in turn, opened the door on a whole range of social and political reforms that led, within 100 years, to a Labour government. This corresponded, in my mind, to the reforms I saw going on in the Catholic church in the wake of Vatican II, the great revival launched by Pope John XXIII in 1962. I got the juvenile idea that history was going my way.

In my last year, I was voted deputy school captain. It actually meant quite a deal to me. Voted by my peers, that sort of thing. I was the Lions club's Youth of the Year for the North-west Coast of Tasmania. No-one was more surprised than me. So I was, at one level, a pretty confident 16-year-old the night a kid came into late study and asked me and another senior boy to come outside and see what Greg had 'done' to a 12-year-old I'll call X. Shivering and distraught, X turned, pulled up his t-shirt and showed us a spray of semen up his back.

I organised three of us to approach a priest I trusted. He advised us to tell the rector, who by this time was Hosie. Three of us went to see him. He expressed no disbelief, not for a moment. Greg was shipped out of the state at year's end, which was only a few weeks later. The two boys and I who had fronted Hosie kept the meeting to ourselves as best we could. Instinctively, we protected the school.

★

In my last year I got a couple of football injuries. Eric offered to give me a rub. We'd developed a bit of a rapport over the years. When I was in the junior dormitory, he'd come in some nights and tell ghost stories. He was of Scottish descent, and living in Scotland in my 20s I heard lots of stories like the ones Eric used to tell – for example, about the man driving the car through the forest at night, seeing a small girl by the side of the road. He stops the car, the child hops in the back, gives her address. When the driver reaches the address, he turns around and is met by an empty seat. She's vanished. The man goes to the door seeking some understanding of this strange event, and an old woman answers. It's the child's grandmother, who says this has happened before. The child was killed in a car accident at the place in the forest where the driver picked her up. His ghost stories alarmed me so much I got scared of walking past the school chapel at night in case the Holy Ghost jumped out at me.

I used to see all the work Eric did around the school and, just quietly, feel sorry for him. One night he told me he'd be glad of death because it would mean an end to all the work. He did everything. The school bus was a clapped-out old Mercedes of a sort otherwise not seen outside Eastern Europe, one that had seating for maybe 18 and regularly carried more. When the bus needed a new engine, Eric put it in. When a school rock band formed, Eric made their amps. Each year, there was a billycart carnival. Eric made the wheels out of synthetic board – hundreds of them. When the sewer blocked, Eric unblocked it. He told me once he'd sooner unblock a sewer than mark maths papers. As a maths and physics teacher, he sat at the front of the class and said exactly nothing. You worked away at problems and, when you couldn't do one, you took it up and Eric showed you what to do. Teaching was when he had a rest.

Eric had a temper – his rage was a force field. Kids treated him with the sort of wary respect you'd show an alpha-male gorilla. One year, maybe my third, Eric was supposed to be leaving. In the end, for whatever reason, he didn't, but in what was supposed to be his last week

I was instructed by a priest to take some message to him in class. Eric said goodbye to me. I was shocked. He said goodbye to me fondly. I saw that he held me in some special regard. My first thought was fear lest any kids in the class had noticed. Being badged Eric's favourite would not be a smart career move.

I saw a sort of Scottish folk tragedy in Eric. When he caned me and said, 'This'll hurt me more than it hurts you,' I believed he meant it. Years later, he said to another former student, 'I didn't want to hit you boys.' He didn't want to but he did and he made it hurt, because, as the discipline master, that was his job. I always had some weird intuition that Eric's mother pushed him into the priesthood, and that reverence to the Church and reverence to his mother were one and the same, that he'd been a totally obedient child which was why he couldn't stand it when kids were disobedient. *He'd always done what he was told ...*

The night Eric gave me the rub, I was in his room. He suggested I take off my pyjama bottoms. I lay on his single bed on my stomach nude from the waist down. He rubbed my legs with oil in what seemed a suitably vigorous and athletic manner. Then I remember him saying, 'If you feel the seed coming, just say.' That struck me as odd, but not alarmingly so. I assumed that he'd said what he had because with some kids it was a possibility. When I rolled over a bit later I saw him quickly look at my cock. It was limp and uninterested. End of story.

The few times I have told this to people, they've cried, 'So you were sexually abused!' I say, 'No, I wasn't.' I've never *felt* I was abused, not then or since. To be abused you must surely feel you've been abused – if someone claims to be offended but feels no offence, that person is a hypocrite. They're merely going through the motions of offence. It has been put to me that my feelings as to whether or not I was abused may be irrelevant in a criminal trial. That's a legal argument I'll leave to lawyers.

I hear survivors of abuse describe similar incidents to my experience with Eric and say it has traumatised them for life. I barely thought about it then; I've barely thought about it since. It has been put to me that having had that experience and not feeling a victim disempowers people who had the same experience and class it as abuse. That is a political argument. I am not seeking to tell a political tale. This is a story about sanity, about getting through this day and then the next one.

I don't think I was abused; my wife, a former school principal with strong views on the subject, thinks I was. About my nude rub with Eric, she said, 'But what if, when you rolled over, you'd had an erection? What would have happened?' Well, yes – different story.

Why did I have the non-response I did? Two reasons, I think. In a TV program about the Pell case, I heard a friend of Pell's accuser, a fellow choirboy from the time, say that part of the trauma for him and his friends was that they believed in the Catholic Church, equating it 'with God and love'. I was never disillusioned by the church because I was never illusioned by it.

The other reason the nude rub may not have affected me as it seems to have affected others is because it was not my first sexual experience. Possibly the only thing I wasn't confused about at the age of 16 was my sexuality. 'The nakedness of woman is the work of God,' wrote the poet William Blake. After being buried alive in an all-male institution for six years, I felt I knew what Blake was on about. The all-male nature of the school depressed me. Women energised me and inspired me to write. They had a magic I craved. I did get moved on one night in a big way by a schoolmate with an enthusiasm for mutual masturbation. I wasn't interested. If I had been, I imagine it would have happened.

★

I remember my last day, six of us in a blue Valiant heading down the drive, cigarette in one hand, beer in the other. It was over. I asked myself what the past six years had meant, opening myself totally to the question, letting any answer appear before my eyes. What appeared was nothing. I interpreted that to mean my schooldays were gone, like men in gangster movies are gone when their feet are set in tubs of concrete and they're dropped overboard into the dark silent waters of a bay.

★

Mum didn't believe me when I got home and told her and Dad about Greg and what he did to the 12-year-old. She got upset and said, 'You'll say anything to discredit the Church.' Dad said nothing but I could see I had him thinking.

My religious war with Mum now entered its climactic phase, with me refusing point-blank to attend Mass. Dad asked me to leave home, saying my views were too upsetting for my mother and grandmother (who lived with us). His request struck me as fair enough.

Mum's response to the news about Greg didn't bother me. I didn't expect her to believe it, given where she had come from. Alongside that, I want to record the fact that when, in my 30s, I was told a story about an eight-year-old coming home from primary school claiming her teacher was stealing sandwiches from the kids' lunches, I didn't believe it. Later, I learnt the teacher had a heroin habit. I didn't believe the eight-year-old because when I went to school, the idea of teachers being heroin users didn't exist as a possibility. I judged accordingly while scarcely recognising the thought process I was employing. When Greg's case finally went to court 30 years after the event, Mum and Dad supported me unequivocally.

People ask me why I don't have resentment towards my parents for sending me to the school. The answer is because I don't. Neither do my two brothers or, for that matter, my sister Mary, who also went to a Catholic boarding school and has many stories to tell. We think our parents did their best for us.

After the age of 10, I only lived at home for two years. When I meet adults trapped in story-cycles about their parents, I often think, 'Your problem is you never left home.' I also bear in mind an old Chinese saying I encountered somewhere along the way: 'Never judge your mother until you have children of your own.' The same would apply to fathers but, interestingly, I don't remember fathers being in the original quote.

During my university years, Dad remained a mystery to me. He was impossible to impress. Nothing I did seemed to matter unless he saw it as bad behaviour and then he'd let me know. Once when I was 18, to get a reaction out of him, I said, 'I'm smoking marijuana.' It was just him and me in the family car, he was driving. There was a moment of silence, then he said, 'Life's about balance.'

One of the few things Dad ever told me about the Burma Railway was that when we were living at Longford in the late 1950s and early 1960s – that is, at a time when Longford was literally as peaceful as any place on earth – he used to think, 'If this is real, the Railway was a dream.' Then he'd think, 'If the Railway was real, this is a dream.' That's a lot to balance, Dad.

★

At school, I was fascinated as much by cricket as football. I still think cricket is a great game – it possesses such variety in terms of the skills required to play it, and is open to so many physical and mental types. As a sport, it is utterly unique, at once both brutal and refined. I played cricket for a number of years after leaving school, but what I gradually moved away from was the culture of the Australian game.

The big turning point for me was the 1974–75 tour of Australia by Mike Denness's England team. Australia had two famously fearsome fast bowlers in Dennis Lillee and Jeff Thomson. Thomson hurled the ball on unpredictable trajectories with an action like a javelin thrower, and publicly stated he liked hitting batsmen. These were the days before helmets and a cricket ball can kill you. The English had no bowler who was anywhere near as threatening. The Australian crowds bayed for blood. It was all too much like bullying for me, and I fell out of love with the Australian team. I don't pretend that this was a rational decision or a considered judgement of the sport. It was like the end of a lot of love affairs – something suddenly wasn't there.

The cricket match where the subversive joke my brother and I share resurfaced to near catastrophic effect was played on a poorly grassed rectangle at the centre of Risdon prison complex. At its eastern end was a high wall painted dog-vomit pink. The whole place was painted dog-vomit pink and known to its inmates as the Pink Palace.

Come the cricket match, the day's sole entertainment, the southern side of the prison was a series of cages with faces pushed up against the bars. When our handsome young fast bowler displayed his naivety by choosing to bowl bare-chested in shorts – as you might in a game of beach cricket – he drew a chorus of wolf whistles and coarse laughter.

Before the match, the captain of the 'home side', an individual doing time for a crime of violence, approached our captain, a senior public servant type, and declared, 'You know how last year you could bowl one bouncer an over – this year we're not having that rule.'

'Goodo,' said our skipper, relieved.

'No,' replied the prison captain with a rush of enthusiasm, 'this year every ball can be a bouncer!'

And it was. There were no helmets and we were three wickets down for less than 10 when I came to the crease. My partner was dismissed a ball or two later. In came Tim. I was playing Tasmanian Cricket Association third grade at the time and experiencing the odd bouncer. Tim wasn't playing cricket at all – his last game had been in our backyard with a tennis ball. The first delivery came straight for his throat.

My brother always has his say. He even managed a

statement of sorts as he leapt in the air and jerked his head away. I ran through for a risky single to get him off strike. In keeping with the uncompromising machismo of the home side, the fielder who picked up the ball attempted the fastest, hardest return in the history of world cricket. It went wildly askew – nearly hitting the square-leg umpire, who ducked and uttered a terrible curse – before going for four overthrows, making my brother our team's top scorer with five. Our team-mates on the boundary rose and clapped as if the score was somehow merited.

Tim gave me the same smirk he'd given me on the altar when I was six, when I discovered the universe has an irresistible comic frequency and, with that, we were in its subversive grip again. He and I, the two batsmen, started snorting with suppressed laughter. The crims thought we were laughing at them like the French legionnaires laugh at death in that old Gary Cooper movie *Beau Geste*. I saw confusion on a couple of faces.

Fortunately for Tim, he was out next ball he faced. As he walked from the wicket, he tapped the ground with his bat like Test batsmen do when they wish to signal that their dismissal was due to a failure of technique or concentration. We both knew it had nothing to do with either. He had reacted from pure, bowel-bursting, squeeze-your-brains-out-through-your-ears, terror. His team-mates clapped him off and he raised his bat to salute them, like Ian Botham did after his historic innings at Headingley in 1981. As we say in sport nowadays, he played a role.

The home side's plan had been to use violence to the fullest letter of the cricketing laws, much as England captain Douglas Jardine did during the Bodyline tour of 1932–33 … and we had laughed at them. The joke was actually about appearances and how totally misleading they can be. They thought we were brave. We thought we were cowards. That was the craziness of the joke and being in the hypermasculine environment of a men's prison fired it with a wild energy.

The aftermath of the joke was like the aftermath of a summer storm, when everything's suddenly different: the smell of the earth, the smell of the air … Plato says courage is knowing what *not* to fear – once the joke settled, I knew not to fear the fast bowler with murder in his eye. I realised he couldn't hit me. He could hurl the ball quickly, but he had no control. He was a right-armed slinger bowling around the wicket. I know this is a bit technical, but I was a right-handed batsman. Tim was a left-handed batsman. The same delivery that could decapitate him passed harmlessly outside my off-stump at a hittable height. I went after the bowler, cutting him square and sending him flying over the slips.

The king of the prison, a man with bulging biceps and a '50s brushback hairdo, was fielding at first slip. I heard him mutter to the wicketkeeper, 'This bloke's tough.'

Me? Tough?!

All I knew was that – in a prison! – I was absurdly free. That I owned the space I stood in. I top-scored with 80-odd, took five wickets with the ball and we won. Highlight of my cricket career. Highlight of Tim's too.

★

I met my first love, a girl my age, in a pub when I was 18. We got serious quickly, nearly wed, then after four years blew apart. Desolate, I spent two years wandering the world, looking for meaning. I had plenty of adventures along the way and was persuaded of the line from Alfred Tennyson's poem 'Ulysses': 'I am a part of all that I have met.' But, after 18 months on the road, I realised I was going nowhere.

Jack Kerouac had defined the promise of the road as 'nothing behind me, everything in front of me'. That was great when I was 13 and there was a lot behind me I wanted to forget and the outside world was an enchanting place, but now there was nothing in front of me either. To borrow from Paul Kelly's song, every fucking city looked the same. I only felt at rest when I was on the move – as soon as I arrived anywhere, I wanted to leave. Deep down, something felt hopelessly wrong. There was a level of meaning I could see in others that I didn't seem to possess. I feared I had lost my soul. On drug trips I saw a shadow following me, getting closer.

My travels ended when I got sick in the Sudan. First day back in Hobart, in a protest march to save a wild river, I met Polly East, a woman I had known at uni and always respected. We'd been good mates, could always sit and talk. She was sensible with drink, I wasn't, having made a sport of sculling. One night we entered an all-male drinking race together as a bit of fun and won, setting a university record. As we got down from the table which served as a sloppy stage, a bloke shouted to Polly, 'You must have balls!' Stopping and turning, she said, 'Why on earth would I want the two things that most distinguish me from you?' I was, I must confess, deeply impressed.

I say Polly's a brave woman – she says she's had to be, being married to me. My reckoning with my boarding-school years came soon after we wed. Polly was expecting our first child and we were living in the green bosom of north-east Tasmania. She loves doing up old houses, and was well underway with her first. The valley we lived in was a picture postcard of rural tranquillity, but I was waking with night terrors. We had everything I could possibly want – an old railway cottage purchased for a paltry $26,000, seven acres of land, seven sheep, and a goat who thought he was human except when he thought he was a sheep … and I was having panic attacks in the night. I'd never had panic attacks before. I would lie awake in a fog of fear – it was like the world was soaked in petrol and I was the one who had to listen for the striking of a match.

★

If what follows reads like it was written in a rush, it's because it happened in a rush. It was as if I had to vomit spiritually, and it took me a few goes to get everything up. I began to doubt everything (but not, thankfully, everyone). What if this sugar I put in my mouth, which everyone assured me was sugar, tasted like salt? What if I looked in a mirror and saw a face not mine? I became preoccupied with death and feared suicide, not because the idea was attractive, but because my mind was accelerating like an out-of-control car and I had no idea where it might go next.

My sister Jo acquainted me with the idea that a first pregnancy can affect male partners in unexpected ways. You're preparing to bring another person into the world for whom you will be responsible, and you're not responsible for yourself. My brother Richard told me he had read a Buddhist text that said when fear grabs you in a formless way, you should ask the fear its name. I asked its name. The answer was boarding school. Could that be true? It was something I rarely thought about.

I wrote a letter to Dad, confiding in him about my turmoil. I'd never told him anything like it before.

He wrote back saying that when they got home from the prison camps they were told to expect feelings of the sort I'd described, but he hadn't had them. It was comforting just to know that other people had feelings of the sort I described – I wasn't as lost, or as alone, as I feared.

One evening, out walking, I actually wondered how I knew that anyone or anything outside me existed. What if everything is just an imagining? What am I? Am I? Years later, I read that Descartes was at a similar point when he declared, 'I think, therefore I am.' I went in the opposite direction, trusting not my intellect, but my senses. Dad had also said he once heard an Anglican clergyman say that life was like feeling your way through a dark room. That was a big clue. I started feeling my way through the dark.

I read eastern philosophy and became acquainted with the idea that if you don't control your mind, your mind controls you. On TV I saw a Vietnam veteran, a man in his 40s permanently shaken by his experience of war, say, 'We were just kids up there.' I got that too – we were just kids at school, kids presented with adult moral dilemmas.

I saw a Winston Churchill quote saying we shape our institutions and then our institutions shape us. I was in an institution for six years. To some extent it made me. Now I had to unmake me. I became deeply immersed in poetry. Poets are the shock troops of language – they can get behind the walls of the mind and liberate thoughts and feelings. The Stephen Spender poem that begins, 'My parents kept me from children who were rough,' has a killer last line: 'I longed to forgive them but they never smiled.' I knew that feeling. A Canadian poet whose name I forget wrote, 'Too soon made a man, too long left a child.' I got that like a catch in the deep.

D. H. Lawrence's poem 'The Snake' describes a key moment in the poet's transition to what he would have called his manhood and I will call his adult uniqueness. The poet sees a snake – his cultural conditioning demands that if he's a man, he'll kill it. 'And voices in me said, If you were a man / You would take a stick and break him.' He flings a rock, the snake slithers off and in that instant the poet experiences a sense of loss. The snake is a thing of wonder and he has banished it from his world by listening to foolish voices in his head that are not him.

I read James McAuley's 'Because'. McAuley was professor of English at the University of Tasmania when I was there in the early '70s. In 'Because', he sees how his parents' emotionally sterile marriage stamped his inner being as a child. The poem ends with him 'descending … Down to that central deadness: the despair / Older than any hope I ever knew.' I realised I'd been living with a central deadness, a despair older than any hope I knew, since I was 13.

★

Each day, to ease the confusion, I recorded images that calmed me or cheered me up. The first was a haiku about a seagull holding its own against a bully wind. Then I wrote this about the dormitory at night, the first thing I'd ever written about school. I was trying to slow down the memory reel so I could see what actually happened back there.

Each Sunday, after evening study,
Forty minutes was devoted to public speaking
(Coarse, vulgar and ungrammatical speech
Will not be used by a boy from this school).
It began with a prayer.

When the priest left the room
And there was no longer
a representative of the order,
they got up a kid who was simple
because it made people laugh.

We closed with a prayer,
returned to the dormitory
and changed in silence.

★

The mental tumult lasted six months, maybe longer. Old things hit me in new ways. One day driving to work it occurred to me that Liverpool fans are correct when they sing, 'Walk on, walk on, with hope in your heart and you'll never walk alone.' Hope's attractive to other people. I was taken with the simple idea that the term 'common sense' implies there are senses we have in common. We are a herd animal – we are not, as Archie Roach once said to me, meant to be alone.

I was like a magpie, taking clues from everywhere. I heard Dad recite a single line from an old Catholic hymn – 'The night is dark, and I am far from home' – and he made it sound grand and solitary and epic. I found the full verse.

Lead kindly light, amid the encircling gloom; Lead
   thou me on!
The night is dark, and I am far from home; Lead thou
   me on!
Keep thou my feet; I do not ask to see
The distant scene – one step enough for me

'Lead kindly light.' I'd met people with a kindly light. 'Amid the encircling gloom.' I knew all about the encircling gloom. 'The night is dark, and I am far from home.' Great line. 'Keep thou my feet.' I knew from footy, you have to keep your feet to stay in the game. 'I do not ask to see / The distant scene – one step enough for me.' Common sense – like the Alcoholics Anonymous pledge about aiming to just stay sober today. Just get through today. One step enough for me.

Witnessing the birth of my daughter Brigid, it struck me that her birth meant the death of a perfectly satisfactory existence in the womb. In birth lies death, in death lies birth. Something inside me was dying to be born.

In the end, one hot day I was standing beside a black-wood tree in the paddock beside our little home, when a shadow hurried across the grass towards me. With it came a great fear that I was about to be extinguished or swallowed up, and I cried out: '*I have a right to be!*'

Pure madness, I know, but I'm glad I did it. Glad I shouted at my shadow. At the negative imprint of those early years. I have a right to be, everybody has a right to be. What do I believe in? Human dignity.

*

This is the second place this book could end.

After the day I shouted at my shadow in the paddock, the confusion was never as deep, never as close to cosmic panic. Thereafter when I went back to school in my dreams, as I often did, the dreams were fantastic – psychedelic, the place a rainbow of colours. I would literally float through the dormitory and into the showers and out again, and there'd be this ecstatic moment when I'd know I was free and that's how I'd wake. Ecstatic, free …

I also found I'd been left with a much clearer idea of what did and did not matter. A whole lot didn't matter to me, but writing did. Through writing I could be part of something nameless and infinitely larger than myself.

I was by now writing for the Launceston *Examiner*. I was also getting the odd poem published. If I had been asked at that time whether I wanted to be a journalist or a poet, I would have said poet, but I found the daily rounds of newspaper life reassuring. I wanted ordinary. I'd taken my walk on the wild side. I wanted sane. Basically, my writing is about sanity.

★

Being paid to be a sportswriter struck me as being the best way imaginable of making a living. I sat in the press box at York Park and looked at the vista to the east – green paddocks, blue hills, the long low shapes of Mount Barrow and Mount Arthur. Bordering the ground were the railway workshops where my grandfather Flanagan and uncles had worked. All the Flanagans were footy people.

I was assigned to ghost-write a weekly column with former Collingwood star Phil Manassa, one of the competition's 'big names'. Phil's fame rested on a goal of great skill and audacity he kicked four years earlier in the 1977 VFL grand final. His critics said it was the only high point of Phil's career. Phil was more than happy to trade insults with his critics but, as a newspaper columnist, beyond expressing his contempt for the standard of Tasmanian football, he had nothing to say. From the outset, Phil made it clear that the less I bothered him – which meant writing what I liked – the happier he'd be.

We both had to tip the winners for each weekend's round on the back page of the Saturday edition. One week, when asked who would win the match between Penguin and Latrobe, Phil replied, 'They're as bad as one a-fuckin-other. They'll draw!' So that's how I recorded Phil's tip in Saturday's paper and – would you believe it? – Penguin and Latrobe drew. Overnight, the column was a sensation.

I never spoke to Phil again, writing the column entirely without him. Phil didn't mind. I even heard on the grapevine that he passed off some of my best lines as his own. I made him a solitary, heroic, Byronic figure given to injudicious but witty asides about other teams and personalities in the competition.

During a game at Smithton, I witnessed a woman fling a well-sauced saveloy at Phil from close range for something I had written under his name. My wife was appalled but the Tasmanian sporting culture I grew up in had a strong element of vaudeville. Phil understood that. He took being struck with the saveloy remarkably well – seeing it, I think, as the actor's lot in the manner of a medieval stage performer dodging rotten vegetables.

For me, sport has always been primarily about fun. Literally, about play. I got Mum to do my tipping and she took to the task with gusto. Latrobe kept losing but she kept tipping them. When I asked why, she said, 'Because Grandad Leary barracked for Latrobe.' Grandad Leary had been dead half a century.

It was all happening. Grandad Leary was tipping from the grave, Phil was the newspaper's celebrity columnist and I reported on a great grand final – Smithton versus Cooee. Matches of stature, which that one was, are like novels with multiple subplots and key moments. I felt the delight any artist feels when gifted a subject that takes them to another creative level. I became aware Dad was reading what I wrote. Writing footy was like writing him a weekly letter.

★

A year or so after I started writing football in Melbourne, Essendon coach Kevin Sheedy named me 'Deepness'. He became interested in me after he learned that I watched matches from the boundary, not the press box. For me to get excited about a game and have words leaping around in my brain like antelopes, I have to feel the pace of the game, the power of the collisions, so that I can better assess the skill and daring. Toward the end of his playing career, Essendon's James Hird – a controversial figure but a sublime player – told me that when he stopped getting excited before a game like he did as a child, he'd stop playing. Same with me as a writer.

Over the years, Sheedy and I had a lot of inter-actions. It was Sheedy who asked me to track down Derek Peardon, Tasmanian Aboriginal footballer and member of the Stolen Generation. I did. The day I gave evidence against Greg, I stood briefly outside the Launceston courthouse talking to the small circle of former students who had come to witness proceedings. After a few awkward exchanges, I hurried off to meet Derek Peardon at a pub of his choice.

We got on in a flash – we were two kids who had used footy to survive institutions. We had squeezed our fun out of it, our sense of a brighter world with all sorts of electricity running through it, and in that boyish way we fitted. Along with his older sister, Peardon had been taken from his distraught mother on an island in Bass Strait and placed in an orphanage for boys in Launceston. His sister, then aged nine, was put in an orphanage for girls some miles away. Every weekend, she crossed Launceston on foot to see her little brother. He was still in the orphanage a decade later when he was equal winner of the best player award at a national Under 16 football carnival. The big clubs came for him. In possibly the first and last time in the history of the game, the decision as to which club he went to was made by the board of an orphanage.

Peardon injured a knee and didn't play many games before disappearing back to Tasmania, but in the short time he was at Richmond he won a place in their champion side of the early 1970s. Kevin Sheedy was in that team. Sheedy is above all curious. He's also a talker. What struck him about Derek Peardon was that he never spoke. All he knew about him was that he was 'an Aborigine'. He was the first Aboriginal person Sheedy had ever met. His fascination with Peardon marked the start of his odyssey into Aboriginal Australia, dragging the game of Australian football behind him and, with it, Australian popular culture.

With time, Sheedy stopped calling me Deepness and called me 'Irishman'. Shortly before he was sacked by Essendon after 26 years and four premierships, I attended a press conference at the Bombers' then home ground, Windy Hill. It was a big deal, lots of TV cameras. Sheedy made a dramatic entry with a couple of club officials. A few steps in he saw me up the back, wheeled and marched to where I stood. Other journalists gathered – was this to be another famous coach/journo showdown? A few inches from my face, he stopped and said, 'Tell me, Irishman – how is it in the land of dreams and visions?' I replied, 'You should know, Kevin.' Nodding, he turned and marched back down to the microphone and invited queries from the so-called real world.

I always say being a footy writer in Melbourne during my time was like being a jazzman in New Orleans. I just loved playing along and was grateful to attract an audience. And what an audience! People who didn't separate sport from art, or sport from music and politics and books, but saw culture – particularly Melbourne culture – as one great pulsating unity.

★

Sport is my major distraction from what I call the real world. To speak of 'the real world' is to invite questions about what is 'real'. In this regard, I am reminded of a story told to me by a New Zealand bikie. He was a wild young man but not violent, and he had gone to hear a Zen guru speak in a bookshop in his native land. A young devotee had sat at the guru's knee and kept inter-rupting when he spoke, crying out, 'But what is real, master? What is real?' Third time he said it, the guru leaned forward and slapped his face. The young man looked astonished. Gesturing to his stinging cheek, the guru said, 'That is real.'

Car crashes are real, so are wars and famine. One of my darkest times followed being confronted with the issue of torture in South Africa in the early 2000s, after I was befriended by a peace worker, a black man tortured by black men in Robert Mugabe's Zimbabwe. I thought torture was an idea banished to the dustbin of history. I would prefer to be killed than tortured – to me, torture is as evil as it gets. Now I saw it coming back, not just politically, but in literary and intellectual circles.

I was fortunate to be allowed to write a 2500-word essay on torture for *The Age*. What happened next unnerved me, because nothing happened. There was no response, just a fearful absence of voices. I heard from four Supreme Court judges who thanked me for what I had written. I saw former Prime Minister Malcolm Fraser, who said in his clipped way, 'I read your essay. It's good – but I think you're too late.' I suddenly saw that history in the 21st century was at serious risk of going backwards, leading to figures like Trump and Putin.

That's when I came across the book that changed my adult life: *Bury the Chains* by Adam Hochschild. It tells the story of the British slave trade, and how it was stopped. Initially, only a handful of people, mostly Quakers, dared to take on the most powerful political and commercial interests in the British Empire at a time when it was the dominant power on the globe.

My very short summary of the book is that the little people won. The football coach voice in my head said, if we won in the past, we can win again. Meanwhile, to my surprise, my *Age* essay on torture, which had seemed to disappear into a black hole of indifference, made it into a global anthology titled *Best Catholic*

Writing of 2006 that included writers of the quality of Mary Oliver and Seamus Heaney. I hadn't won, but, in one small sense, I hadn't lost. I'd had my say.

I believe my old school helped shape me as a journalist. It taught me what not to fear and gave my ambition a hard edge. To better explain, I'm calling a witness – Paul O'Halloran – to describe how it made him an activist.

★

In June 2021, with five other former players from the Tasmanian University Football Club, Paul and I protested against the proposed construction of a tailings dam in the Tarkine rainforest in south-west Tasmania. Of the seven old footballers, three had divorced, one was a widower of many years who had never re-partnered, and one was in a long-standing gay relationship. But the one who immediately struck me as having changed was Paul.

He says as a young man – which is when I knew him – he was timid and shy. That's pretty much as I remember him. He's now a citizen of the planet who's fearless in his tread. When I asked him how that change came about, he talked about the old school.

In later life, trying to untangle the logic of his curious but colourful existence, T. E. Lawrence (better known as Lawrence of Arabia) invented a new word:

'school-fear'. It's a good word – I can smell it. In my first three years, and to a diminishing extent in my fourth, I knew school-fear on a daily basis, a grey rawness in your guts. Paul recalled how we had class diaries and we used to number off the days and hours and minutes until we were free to go home inside them. His home was a farm cut out of forest in the island's far north-west.

The two priests he says imposed themselves upon him sexually at school were Groucho and Tom. His brother Steve's allegations were against Tom and Herman. The O'Halloran brothers reached a settlement with the order that ran the school, but Paul's not stopping. He doesn't believe justice has been fully done. It was Paul's lobbying that got the Royal Commission into Institutional Sexual Abuse to come to Tasmania.

There are a number of differences between Paul's story and mine. Paul was good at sport. Three weeks after he arrived at the school as an 11-year-old, he top-scored with 74 not out to give our school a rare victory. Cricket was emblematic of the private-school system and we were notoriously poor at it, but, in 1965, in what seemed momentous at the time, we defeated Scotch at Scotch, with 13-year-old Paul, then in Year 9, top-scoring with 34. He told me he concentrated so hard he got a migraine.

To play in the First XI in Year 9 was most uncommon. In Year 10, he played for the First XVIII. That too was unusual, and it also happened to be by far the best football team the school had in my time, winning the state premiership on our muddy home ground in a match televised around the state. Paul was three years ahead of me. When I saw him, he was always surrounded by other boys but he was friendly. A smile from a big kid – particularly if he was popular and good at sport – was the sunshine in a little kid's day.

Another difference is that Paul started school as a believer of sorts. By the time he reached Year 12, however, his political side had started to kick in. He decided religion was a hoax aimed at social control, particularly over women, but said nothing. He wasn't bullied at school – he was too popular – but he witnessed the power of groups, saw how individuals could be made to wither before your eyes, and feared it. He was so nondescript in his demeanour he didn't get a nickname. He also couldn't speak to women.

That all changed in his fourth year at university when he had his first 'serious' relationship and simultaneously got involved in Vietnam War protests. He was active in the great Tasmanian environmental battles of the '70s and '80s. The more political he became, the more outspoken he was. Then came woodchipping, which was about felling rainforests like the ones he'd grown up among. For three years, he sat as a Green in the Tasmanian parliament.

Paul says school was the worst time of his life. Me,

too. He became a science teacher and believes the aim of education is to open minds. 'We were trampled into submission. Even a good kid like me got 20 to 30 cuts a year. You walked around being scared by bullies in authority.' Remember a story I told earlier about Herman ordering an entire classroom not to look out the window when a truck pulled up outside the school? Paul O'Halloran glanced. I can imagine the rest – Herman leading the terrified kid ceremonially to his office, Herman who could split a pillow with his cane. That's something Paul and I share: we both experienced the terror that was Herman.

When we went into the Tarkine, we took a shiny new Sherrin football. We had to get past two gates and two lots of security guards. The guard at the first gate spotted the Sherrin and cried out, 'You can't bring that in here!' In keeping with the finest traditions of the Australian game, he kept his eyes on the ball and we slipped past. We were five or six k's down the track when two cop cars appeared and apprehended us. The cops were genial, but one of them led Paul away to tell him that the security guard, the one who tried to arrest the footy, was alleging Paul had assaulted him by driving his car into him. Paul wasn't having it. He talked back. There was no fear of authority in him (fear of authority is something I can smell).

Paul O'Halloran's story is about the timid schoolboy who became an outspoken 70-year-old. And this is something else Paul and I share, something else we know in the core of our beings. If you get knocked off your line when you're young in a way that causes you to forfeit self-respect and in its place feel self-loathing, it can make you defend your integrity in later years like your life depends on it. From the time I started working in newspapers, I didn't tolerate people interfering with my work for reasons I didn't respect. I wasn't having my name on anything that wasn't me, a position I held to tenaciously but with ease, having experienced the bitter remorse that comes from being compromised by others and acting against your own true nature at the old school.

*

I arrived at *The Age* in 1985 like a young man from the provinces of north Africa arriving in Imperial Rome, the centre of the known world. The place was brimming with talent: writers, artists, photographers, cartoonists. It had been described the previous year by an English writer as one of the 12 best English language newspapers in the world. *The Age* dominated classified advertising, had lots of cash and thought little of sending a journalist across the world in pursuit of a story they deemed important.

The editor was a World War II veteran called Creighton Burns, who'd been both an academic and a former Washington correspondent. I had been at *The Age* three months when I was sent to interview Weary Dunlop, the hero of the Burma Railway. When I returned to the office, Creighton stopped by my desk, as editors then were wont to do, and asked me what my story was that day. I told him and added, 'My father was with him during the war.' Creighton replied, 'Do you want to go [to Thailand]?' Three weeks later, I was standing in Hellfire Pass, where most of the Australians had perished.

Each day, I went places my mysterious father had been with men who had been there with him. Each night I went to Weary's room, drank whisky and got him telling stories. Here's one of the stories he told me:

Thailand, 1943. He's dealing with an array of tropical diseases and a captor literally prepared to work its prisoners to death. He has a hidden wireless. The guards know but can't find it. He's betrayed. In a cell awaiting a horrible death by bayoneting he realises … he's not as scared as he was as an 11-year-old standing outside the headmaster's door.

That's me! That's me outside Herman's door! I know what this man — maybe the bravest I've ever met — is talking about.
Realising he isn't as scared as he was as a kid outside the headmaster's door, Weary finds himself recalling

Keats' 'To Autumn', which, he says, 'I knew quite well at school.' He recites it to me in the grand manner used by people who grew up with poetry before the invention of radio and recorded music. It's like hearing a magnificent old elephant trumpeting at night through the jungle.

*

The Jesus I knew at school was totally humourless. The chapel was a zone of enforced reverence, and Eric and Booze were the chief enforcers. The high priest of seriousness – the Boris Karloff of the genre – was Herman.

I contrast these memories with a meeting I had with Archbishop Desmond Tutu in a café in Cape Town in the 2000s. I had long been taken with Tutu's raucous cackle of a laugh and how it kept bubbling out of him. During the apartheid years, I'd seen footage of him diving into a black crowd to save a suspected police informer being 'necklaced' – having a rubber tyre placed around their necks, filled with petrol and set ablaze.

This day in the café, he was sitting with a dozen or so people and once or twice I'd heard the cackling laugh. He got up to leave alone and I caught him at the door. He turned and I wasn't prepared for the immense weariness I saw in his face. I pressed on, asking the question I'd always wanted to ask him. 'Does God laugh?' He took my forearm solemnly in his hands and said, slowly and with emphasis, 'Yes, my friend. God laughs – and God cries,' and I saw within him, as deep as a mineshaft, where despair had taken him.

South Africa is the most dramatic place I've been. You see the lot, good and bad, in a naked, obvious way. In South Africa, I got seriously scared by the evil of torture and in South Africa I saw that hope, like love, can be made.

Most people in western culture, when asked if they have hope, answer by employing reason. They find reasons to hope or not to hope. Black South Africans get together, find a beat and a hearty chorus emerges and the more people that join in, the greater the joy, because you're not alone. You're part of the vibe, the vibe is part of the place and so on. It's akin to the Zen proverb every good footy coach knows: 'Feeling discouraged? Encourage another.'

★

Someone once said to me, 'You must have met a lot of bullies working in sport and the media.' But I didn't, or, if I did, I hardly noticed. The people I most respected in footy encouraged me. And I didn't meet anyone like Herman or Jagger. It was years before anyone scared me as much as they had and that individual was a real-life gangster.

In some ways, after I left school it seemed I had a charmed existence. Like when I hitchhiked into Belfast in the 1970s during the civil war, arriving at dusk. The Protestant truck driver who'd given me a lift was due home for one of his kids' birthdays – instead, he was in a phone box, calling around, trying to find me a safe place for the night. And so, as fate would have it, Irish Protestants – the people history said were my enemy – protected me from one side of the troubled province to the other.

Ireland, and Northern Ireland, was a big restart for me. I began to understand that what I was seeking didn't have a name – it didn't have a label like a religion or nationality – but my biggest travel experience happened after I got back to Australia and entered Aboriginal Australia. History said I was their enemy but, overwhelmingly, they didn't treat me that way. I thought that their culture, however troubled, had soul. And I kept meeting Aboriginal people who seemed to understand exactly what I was doing and why. You could say, to borrow a Catholic idea, that they confirmed me in my path.

Twice as a journalist I got involved in dangerous stories. The one with the gangster gave me nightmares. Polly doesn't like being woken at night and, after three months of that occurring, she'd had enough, shaking me awake with the words, 'You're having another nightmare!' I said, 'They're chasing me.' She said, 'Well, you chase them for a fucking change.' So I did. The nightmare vanished and never returned.

★

Who should contact me after a few years at *The Age*, but Booze. The old bastard who caned kids like he was giving them their just desserts, but who also, as a teacher, opened my mind. Booze, I now gathered, followed my writing. We arranged to meet one night and go for something to eat. Seeing him walking up the street with his curious waddle, I thought, 'Is this old man the person I feared like the wrath of a vengeful God?'

We went to a Greek restaurant, had a few drinks, and talked amiably enough. I remember Booze saying, 'Alcohol can be a friend.'

Next time we met a year or so later, I turned up with an armful of friends – six long-neck beers. Booze, by now well into his 70s, had been sent back to the town where the old school is as a parish priest. I don't know how drunk he got, but I know my boat slipped its moorings.

I said what I thought of his religion; not rudely, but in the spirit of a frank discussion. He didn't like it. I saw the redness in his face intensify and that glint in his eyes that told you that you were in deep shit. I'm embarrassed to admit it but I felt this weird compulsion to go over, kneel down and ask him to hear my confession. That if I did, a great love would overwhelm me and welcome me into its midst. Fortunately, I'd had drug trips in which weird thoughts had surfaced and I'd learnt to last them out. Putting the strange effect down to the local beer, I held – politely, I hope – to my views. We never saw one another again.

★

In 1993, my novel *Going Away* appeared. It's based on the two years I spent wandering the world looking for something, not knowing what. The book cuts back to boarding school years and tells some of the stories told herein, but not all, because I didn't want to upset Mum.

In the event, she was upset by *Going Away*. I'd written how exciting it was when kids pissed off. A girl boarder had run away when she was at a Catholic boarding school in Hobart in the 1920s and the nuns made them pray for the escapee, filling their heads with images of what could befall a young woman on the streets of Hobart at night. Mum got over what I had written soon enough, and it was never mentioned again. The last time I spoke to her about the religious differences we had when I was a kid, she couldn't remember them, and seemed surprised that any such thing had occurred.

Essentially, *Going Away* is a jig, a reel, a series of stories spun in a certain spirit. I dedicated the book to

Bob Brown and Archie Roach, two men of my generation who'd been to the pit of despair and worked their
way out – one through nature, one through music.
Archie autographed my copy and wrote inside the
cover, 'To see yourself, to lose yourself, to see yourself
anew – that is the journey.'

The Australian newspaper handed *Going Away* to
a former Jesuit priest, who gave me a verbal caning.
He opened with something like: 'Certain people in
Melbourne (intelligent people) have advised me that
this man is the best sportswriter in Australia. I must be
the only person in Australia not interested in sport but,
having read his novel, I suggest he goes back to writing
it. His novel is a collection of stories that adds up to
nothing.'

Nothing.

That word again. I was back in the dormitory aged
13, terrified by the emptiness of the night. I'd spent 25
years writing my way out of *nothing*, and now the words
were said to add up to … nothing.

I spoke to a black brother up on the Murray River.
He and I had quite a back story, dating back to a sacred
object I had returned to his country. He took the review
personally, and saw it as an attempt to steal my spirit
(which is what it actually felt like). He said, 'Come up
here, brother, we'll smoke ya, we'll protect ya from that
shit.' I never got hurt by a critic after that.

What I learnt was that the weight of any compliment

or criticism is in direct proportion to the respect you have for the person making it.

★

1997. I'm at a pre-match function in the committee room of the Melbourne Cricket Club. The Swans are playing the Dogs. The lunch compere introduces me to the room. I'm eating first course when a bloke with a shiny bald head appears at my elbow. He's kneeling, slightly hesitant in manner.

He says, 'We went to school together.'

I'm pretty good with faces; I can't remember him.

'Paul McMahon,' he says.

The name doesn't ring a bell. I don't like to disappoint but I'm about to.

'Rinso,' he says.

Flashlights go off in my head like a press conference when the superstar enters. Rinso?! How could I forget Rinso? I was there the day he was bashed. He's a Bloods supporter now. I saw plenty of blood on him that day, a big red V down the front of his white shirt.

Rinso and I watched the game together. He lives in Sydney and is a successful businessman who set up one of the Swans' major sponsorships. We spoke and watched the game, watched and spoke. Then, in that special way that happens when you're at the footy, not looking one another in the eye, I said quietly, 'I was there the day Chris bashed you,' and he replied just as quietly, without looking across, 'I knew someone was watching.'

And I felt it again, the terrible loneliness of being a witness to a bashing. *My God, my God, why have you forsaken him?*

Rinso left the MCG early. When he'd gone, a man came across, and sat beside me. He was in a curious state, agitated almost. Rinso had told him about our exchange. The man said his son was having trouble with bullies at school. He was Rinso's boss and he said Rinso was the most principled man he'd ever met.

That day, I was astounded to learn that Rinso – the last person I expected it from, given the bashing – had started visiting Tasmania from Sydney and looking up fellas he went to school with. I didn't know anyone doing anything like that as far as the old school was concerned. I put him in touch with Tim. The next thing I knew, Rinso was staying at Tim's place and they were friends.

★

Where does the story of my school years end? It doesn't. The schoolbook for 1966, my first year, has a photo of the school band. I am the 11-year-old standing at the end of the middle row, cornet angled ceremoni-ally across my chest. Behind me stands a boy four years older also holding a cornet ceremonially angled across his chest. His name is James Griffin. He committed suicide in 2020 after an inquiry unearthed that he had engaged in decades of paedophilic activity while working as a hospital nurse in Launceston. I know little of his case, but my first thought learning of it was to wonder if something happened to him at school. You have to wonder.

From a third party, I hear that a kid who slept across from me in the junior dormitory, our heads maybe 40 centimetres apart, had told him a story that one night he was woken by a priest and taken with another boy to a room where they were incited to wank, while a couple of priests watched. Does this sound true to me? No. Can I say it didn't happen? No.

More recently, a fella I knew quite well at school tells me of finding a kid about to hang himself in the stairwell next to the chapel. I know the stairwell – a lonely, half-dark, loop of concrete steps. The kid who was about to hang himself was obviously gay. Can I say that story's true? No. It's hearsay. Can I imagine it? Only too well.

With each new shock revelation in the media, I return to school in my head. I know my brothers do too. 'Do you believe the stuff about Herman?' I ask Tim. The ABC story on the O'Halloran brothers says there are now four complaints against him. 'It makes you wonder,' he replies.

How the priests dispensed corporal punishment said a lot about them. Booze gave it like all boys need a good thrashing like they need three meals a day and a roof over their heads. Eric did it because it was his job to hurt you and, regretfully, he did. There was another priest who did it with humour and didn't hit you very hard – an altogether different experience and trivial by comparison to, say, the experience offered by Herman.

Pain is like sex in its power to transform relationships. They both speak a deep non-verbal language. I once met a former Jesuit who told me he got out of the priesthood because he found that caning kids was giving him an erection. I could only say I respected him.

*

Pat, my oldest brother, is the quietest and most conservative of us. Last time I asked him if he was still a Catholic, he said wearily, 'Just.' He has been working with the homeless in Hobart in one capacity or another, mostly as a volunteer, for over 50 years. He visits old people who are dying who have no other visitors. He's what is known in Yiddish as a 'mensch', in the old Australian vernacular as a good bloke.

Pat started at the old school in 1960, its second year of operation. In its first year, there was only one class or year level – in the second year, there were two, the third year three etc. It meant he was always one of 'the big kids'. On the subject of sexual abuse, with a tone of some bemusement, he shakes his head and says, 'I didn't see or hear anything.' Sometimes he wonders if he was deaf and blind.

Two fellas from my time who have read this manuscript say similar things. I don't disbelieve them just as they don't disbelieve me. Our school was solitary in a way which anyone who hasn't grown up outside their family is unlikely to understand. You were intimately known and intimately unknown, both at once, every minute of every day. Another fella said to me he didn't mind school because the priests weren't as cruel as his father.

Pat took four weeks to get back to me after reading this manuscript. When he did, he said 10 words: 'I think you went into things I stayed out of.' Upon reflection, I suspect that's true. I always wanted to see what was going on, being a journalist by nature.

I once spoke at a conference in Melbourne with a gay Irishman who had spent five years in a seminary studying to be a priest. He said there were Irish academic studies which showed that sexual abuse took off during the 'permissive years' of the 1960s – the era when society was reverberating to calls for sexual freedom. A new 'vibe' was in the air. A new history was dawning and it must have seemed to some of the young men who had entered the priesthood on the basis of

1950s belief systems that they were at risk of being left behind like relics of a former age. If there was a new freedom in the world, why not some freedom for them? Suppressed energy leaks out in other ways. A fella from the old school once sent me a photo of a car sticker that read: 'Abstinence Makes The Church Grow Fondlers.' (Unlike some, I don't believe the Catholic Church has had a monopoly on sexual abuse. They just did it in their own uniquely fucked-up way.)

The school changed so much during my time – 1966 to '71. The priests stopped wearing cassocks and clerical collars. Suddenly they looked like drink waiters in black trousers and white shirts with small gold crosses pinned to their collars. We had guitars in Mass instead of the organ. Guitars were the instruments of folk music, of the protest movement. As a reluctant altar boy, I had been forced to learn the Latin Mass. Suddenly, the Latin Mass was as extinct as the dinosaur. Half a dozen of the priests I knew at school left the priesthood within a decade and married. The future of a much more liberal Catholic Church seemed as certain as next summer.

In 1968, we got a radical priest who openly and unapologetically supported the anti-Vietnam War movement. He fired us up about the mass student revolts in Paris. That same year a kid called Peter Rowe led a walk-out over the food which was unspeakably bad. Eric was volcanic. He got us in a room and hissed, 'If I knew the name of the boys who organised that walk-out, I'd punch their teeth into the pit of their bellies.' One of the priests later said he feared for the radical priest that day because he thought Eric might drop him.

★

Peter Rowe and I talk on the phone 54 years after the Great Food Walk-Out, 54 years after we last saw each other. He's had two careers, first as a teacher, then as a lawyer. He tells his stories slowly, in phrases, each one edged with a faint but persistent humour.

As a kid, he was a believer, an altar boy. He attended the big Christian Brothers school in the south. 'I was utterly submissive to the staff and other students who were less humane than they were at our school.' That was his first thought when he arrived at our school. How lucky we were.

He describes our old school as 'thin' academically. 'They had no science block until 1965. There was no woodwork or metalwork. There was sport but there was no physical education. There was no art, no music program beyond the band.' There were cadets, but the Commonwealth government paid for them.

When he got to our school, for the first time, he saw priests close up. 'Familiarity breeds contempt. I used to have priests up on a pedestal. I realised they were human. They were flawed, some were deeply flawed – as am I.'

In his third year at our school, his religion teacher was Father Hargreaves, the priest Tim and I liked best. Peter says he was becoming gradually more disillusioned with the religion but hadn't abandoned it yet. Hargreaves introduced him to a magazine for young Catholics that asked open-ended questions about their faith. 'The Catholic Church had taught me to be judgemental. I don't think they expected me to be judgemental about them.' Hargreaves had a quiet word with him, saying he might be better off at a government school.

In his term 1 report for 1968, the year of the Great Food Walk-Out and Peter's final year, Bernard Hosie wrote, 'Peter definitely has the interests of the school at heart.' Peter says, 'The school should've had my interests at heart. I wasn't building the place.'

Over the course of 1968, 'My relationship with the management became increasingly confrontational. I outgrew the school's command and control system.'

This same year the school had conducted an experiment in student leadership, replacing the prefect system with a Student Representative Council. Within one year, Peter Rowe, an SRC member, was seen to have led a revolt, although he says the walk-out was not his idea. It was just that the kid whose idea it was didn't walk.

I was surprised to learn that Peter didn't hear Eric's famous 'I'd punch their teeth into the pit of their bellies' speech, delivered that evening to an audience of blood-drained faces. That's because Bernard Hosie had called a meeting of the SRC and told them to hand their badges in.

I have a strong memory of Peter Rowe being caned that year by a priest I'll call Father Black. It was totally without precedent for a kid on the SRC or a prefect to be caned. I was next kid in to Black's office, so I listened as he got four lusty cuts. Then the door opened and I heard him say to the priest, man to man, 'This is bloody ridiculous.'

He finished at the school at the end of that year. On his very last day, he was with a kid who pulled out a cigarette and lit up in the dormitory. He offered Peter a drag. 'I had a puff. It was the first cigarette of my life.' Who should walk in but Eric.

Peter was the ringleader of the walk-out. The night the six kids got six cuts each, the kid who had to wait until last and suffer the most was, I am pretty sure, the one Eric thought was the ringleader.

Peter tells the story this way: 'He invited me to go round to his room to get the cuts. I said, "No. I'm leaving." He said, "You won't get a reference from this school." I said, "It wouldn't be much of a reference, would it?"'

For speaking truth to power – I only saw one other kid do it to anything like the same extent – and for making a stand on behalf of the rest of us, Peter Rowe is high on my honour board, up near the top.

★

In 1985, when I went back to the Burma Railway with Weary Dunlop and a group of old diggers, one of the group pulled me aside when we were in Hellfire Pass, where they had suffered so much and many had died. He wanted to tell me a story about Dad. One night during the monsoon, the guards came round the tents saying that one man from every tent was required to pull out a Japanese truck that had bogged. Dad was a sergeant. He could have ordered someone else to go, but went himself. That was the story.

I returned home and told Dad. He said, 'Not true.' He always dismissed stories where people spoke well of him. Unusually for me, I pressed him. This wasn't pub talk, I said. This was the testimony of someone who witnessed an event, told to me in the place where it had occurred. I saw him process what I said. It was like he went back into the courtroom of his mind, returning after some minutes to say, 'I have no memory of it.' At that moment I realised he preferred truth to illusion in a radical, not to say eastern, way.

I always say that if Dad had been a sly grog merchant, he would have dealt in whisky – he was the great distiller. After his experience of the prison camps, he distilled Christianity to three phrases: 'I was hungry and you fed me, I was naked and you clothed me, I was in prison and you visited me.'

After Roger was sent to Hobart's Risdon prison in 2007, my brother Pat began visiting him. After Greg was found guilty and sentenced, in part on my evidence, Tim visited him. My brothers didn't do these things because they thought the priests were innocent. They did it because they thought that if they didn't visit them, no-one would. Some people didn't like them doing it. I'm proud of my brothers.

★

My brother Richard directed my parents' funerals. Having previously directed a movie of one of his novels, he was well suited to the task. Both were great occasions. Mum's funeral was followed by a wake at Richard's place, a riot of voices and music and laughter ringing out into the night. Dad's funeral was more sombre.

What moved me most at Dad's funeral was a telegram sent by four Japanese women, members of the Japanese peace movement, who had flown to Hobart to meet him five or so years earlier. They had all grown up with versions of their country's involvement in World War II, which they had discovered post-war to be false and were now actively seeking historical truth. My brother Pat had met them during a visit to Japan. On learning Dad's story, they asked if Dad would meet with them if they flew out to Tasmania.

It was a big drama for him, a big weight. The men who died on the Burma Railway stayed with him to the end. He'd talk to them in the backyard each evening at sunset when he looked to be attending to menial garden chores. He told me the men who had died would see him meeting the Japanese women as fraternising with the enemy. Nonetheless, he did it.

I was present when they arrived and there was a period when no-one could get into the house because neither side had an appropriate ritual for doing so. When they did get in, they all sat around the kitchen table and talked. In the telegram they sent to the funeral, the Japanese women said Dad had a noble mind and was 'objective about his suffering' – that is, he understood the suffering of the Japanese people also, particularly from the atomic bombs and the firebombing of Tokyo.

During their final years I took it in turns with my siblings to live with Mum and Dad and look after them. I spent days with Dad where neither of us spoke a word. He didn't want to; I didn't want to make him. I did ask him how he felt about dying. He said, 'I don't worry about it.' After that, I didn't worry about it either.

Mum lived long enough to see Richard win the Man Booker literary prize for his novel *Narrow Road to the Deep North*. She knew he had won it weeks earlier. How she knew, we never understood. At one point her vital signs ebbed and faded, and it was thought she had passed away. Then she revived. Asked how she felt, she cried, 'Elated! Richard's won the prize!' A few weeks later when he actually did win, she received the news as calmly as if she were being told the neighbour had a new dog.

Mum went out like a rock star, lots around her bed – kids, grandkids, great-grandkids, everybody talking, half-a-dozen conversations criss-crossing the room like buzzing telephone lines. Mum went out listening to the craic. Her last words were, 'Thanks, everyone, I've had a lovely time.'

*

In 1993, *The Age* was taken over. The new owner, Canadian-born businessman Conrad Black, later did time in an American prison for fraud, before being pardoned (after his release) by his former business partner Donald Trump. In the build-up to the take-over, I had been on the back of a truck in Treasury Gardens with former prime ministers Gough Whitlam and Malcolm Fraser, campaigning for the newspaper's independence. Soon after the new regime was installed, I was taken aside by a section editor. He said there was 'a view' that I ran around doing what I liked and wrote about people 'too glowingly'.

Fighting words. I'd travelled the world alone, I'd worked in a prison – I thought I was entitled to my view of human nature. I asked my accusers in what case had I excluded evidence that was damaging to the subject of a story? No reply. I asked, in what case had I presented evidence in a false or misleading manner? No reply. I started being told what stories were before I began investigating them. I think stories start where your preconceptions end.

It was a protracted battle. One highlight was Paul Kelly opening a concert at St Kilda Beach in front of 14,000 people, saying, 'This next song is for my friend Martin Flanagan, who's going in on Monday to tell them they can ram their job up their arse.' (The song was 'Little Boy Don't Lose Your Balls'.) I'd seen Paul backstage before the show. He asked how I was. I told him, he told 14,000 people. After the show I informed him that up until the moment he told the 14,000, Polly was the only other person who knew.

Eventually, the dispute was settled. It was agreed that if a story carried my name, the words which appeared beneath my name were mine. If the people running the paper didn't want me to write on a subject, they shouldn't ask me to.

After that, if I could avoid it, I didn't go back into the building. I once said to a woman who worked for the Catholic Church, 'In newspapers, the enemy is always in the building.' She said, 'It's the same in the Catholic Church.' I see clerics like George Pell as the Vatican equivalent of those senior Soviet bureaucrats who lined up each year behind supreme leaders like Leonid

Brezhnev for the annual May Day Parade, all wearing the same hat, the same overcoat, the same expression on their faces, all making out that their lives were devoted to guarding the spirit of the revolution when the spirit of the revolution was long gone.

★

Only connect, said EM Forster of writing. I love connecting in the way that some people love the dance floor. One of my best experiences as a hitchhiker was getting into a car in a foreign land, having no language in common with the driver. Then, with the passage of time and lots of different scenery going past the window, you begin to read his manner and know you like him. What's more, you know he likes you, and that's all you need to have a good time on the road.

I loved connecting with Aboriginal people. No-one taught me more, not just about relating to the earth, but about stories, how they have to be done 'proper way' or you distort them and get them wrong. Encountering Jews, Muslims, Hindus, I rejoiced in the universal qualities I beheld.

Three Catholic ceremonies I attended over the years connected me. The first was a vigil held at Saint Ignatius church in the Melbourne suburb of Richmond at the very moment a local parishioner, 25-year-old Van Tuong Nguyen, was hanged in a Singapore jail for drug running. He was executed at eight o'clock in the morning. It was my daughter Brigid's idea for us to go.

If ever a silence was deathly, it was the quiet of that church during the young man's last half-hour as the minute hand ticked upwards. A few minutes before 8 am, the warders came and got him. It was impossible not to accompany the young man on his walk to the gallows. I was struck that day by the thought that Christianity is a religion born of a state execution.

The second ceremony was Ned Kelly's funeral in a Catholic church in Wangaratta in January 2013. An unlikely connection involving Ned had been suggested to me a couple of years earlier during a visit to Israel with the AFL Israeli Palestinian Peace team. We'd gone to the synagogue in Nazareth where Jesus, having gone out of his senses in the desert fighting temptation, returned to make the first of his messianic utterances. The locals took it badly and dragged him to a cliff to throw him off. Our Israeli guide said Jesus escaped by flying to another mountain. I hadn't read the gospels since I'd done Religious Knowledge with Roger and Booze, but that didn't ring a bell.

Reg Saunders, a great Gunditjmara man I was fortunate to meet along the way, once said to me, 'Stories are most powerful in the place they're from.' Reg had gone to Palestine as an Australian soldier during World War II – that was where he had visualised the Jesus story. In a Tel Aviv market, I bought a second-hand Bible and read the New Testament in the place the stories come from. I read again where he told the young man to leave his father's funeral and follow him then and there – it struck me as the action of someone who didn't know who his real father was. But what also struck me was his courage.

I visited the Garden of Gethsemane where he prayed to quell his terror. I climbed the hill where he carried the plank he was to be nailed to. He could have got away but chose to walk towards his fate. I was reminded of another fearless young rebel from my culture who could have got away but chose to walk towards his fate also. There the similarities end, but it was as if by knowing one, I knew the other better.

The bikies on the door at Ned's funeral grunted, 'No media!' It was the first time I'd seen bouncers on a church door. An old nun smuggled me in through the back. How much of Ned was at the funeral? His skull, hacked from the flesh in which it was encased, was last seen in West Australia, according to the man claiming to be its owner. In the 1890s, a Melbourne lawyer boasted of using Ned's scrotum as a tobacco pouch.

Ned's coffin was parked halfway up the aisle, as if it wasn't sure it should get too near the altar. Draped on the coffin was the green sash he was given for saving a kid from drowning when he was 12. He wore the sash beneath his armour when he stepped out of the mist and marched on the small army of police and native troopers to draw their fire and enable his brother and two other companions to escape the Glenrowan Hotel where they were trapped.

From where I sat, a large wooden cross on the far wall – one with no human figure attached – appeared to touch the lid of the coffin and the sash. The merging of the symbols brought a rock-hard reality to the funeral, as at the prayer vigil for Van Tuong Nguyen.

The third Catholic ceremony that connected with me was run by my old school at the start of 2021 and called A Ritual of Lament.

★

I have it in my head that if Booze read this book, he'd say, 'Martin is too emotional.' That if Biggles read it, he would call out, 'Don't exaggerate, Flaps,' and I would hear some of the older boys laugh. That the priest running the infirmary that day in second year, maybe Roger, would say I was 'putting it on'. And, at some level, I'd believe each of them. Why? Because they were the adults, larger examples of the same species – like bigger, older monkeys with smaller, younger monkeys. In that elementary way, you looked up to them.

Eric would feel wounded and betrayed by what I've written about the nude rub. I can only say that I subjected my memories to the same test I applied before giving evidence against Greg. I make the point that Eric didn't hurt me and, on this occasion, didn't scare me. I never felt the situation was out of my control, nor did I ever hear another story about Eric of that type. Over the years, Eric stories have continued to be told, but they're about his temper and potential for violence. If I could travel back in time to those days, I'd say to Eric, 'Get out, mate. I can't promise you happiness, but I can tell you that your life doesn't have to be this lonely.'

I am very interested in Irish writer Samuel Beckett. I feel like I live in a country that neighbours the one he writes about. If I wrote my version of Beckett's play *Waiting for Godot*, the stage would be a charmless school chapel like the one we had – varnished hardwood pews, flaking plaster saints all north European in appearance, not a Semite in sight. The script would be a sermon delivered by a young priest who still possesses a vestige of idealism and belief. He has to believe he's doing God's work, his sanity demands it, but he also knows the only reason the kids aren't rioting in the pews is because they're too scared, that the presence in his church is not the bright hope of a loving God but fear.

Eric later went to Pakistan. I read an account of his time there written by a fellow priest. It seemed an authentic appraisal. Eric's great achievement was inventing and building an ingenious hot-water system for the local nuns. It noted that the school he was assigned to had no discipline problems, the kids all being talented and from rich ambitious families. No discipline problems. That was the difference. Kids misbehaving drove Eric nuts. *The ingratitude of it!*

I see a lot of Irish-Australian Catholic priests from that time as having been pushed into it by their families. For poor Irish-Australian Catholic parents, of whom there were a lot at one time, having a priest in the family was like being connected to royalty. As an old Irishman I worked with on a garbage truck in London in the '70s said to me, as he fell backwards pissed from our truck: 'There are many kings but only one Pope!' Mum had a cousin who entered a seminary but abandoned it and came home. His parents kept praying that he would rediscover his vocation. He ended up going back to the seminary and 20-odd years later was convicted of indecent assault on a male.

One man who read this manuscript declared, 'Priests are rapists!', meaning, as I understood him, that all priests are rapists. When people generalise about priests in a negative way, I ask, if we agree that making negative generalisations about groups of people is wrong, then surely making negative generalisations about priests is wrong?

Were there priests at my school who were conscientious? I thought so. Moreover, they worked unpaid in an all-male environment not much different from a prison. The idea of finding myself trapped in such a place as an adult horrifies me. It would mean inhabiting a forest of meaningless symbols underlaid with a terrible haunting emptiness. I wouldn't last a day. When Greg was found dead in the Sydney unit where he lived alone at the age of 84, my first thought was, 'What a sad, hopeless life.'

Did the other priests know what was going on in the rooms of Greg and Tom? Two of the priests whose integrity I have no cause to question have stated – one to Tim, another to a mutual acquaintance in Melbourne – that they didn't. A former member of the order also told me the priests at the school did not, as some have speculated, hear one another's confessions (the implication being that they were thereby informed of any sexual misconduct). I've heard cynics say none of the priests believed in the confidentiality of the confessional, but I don't believe what I witnessed during my six years in the school was one long display of cynical behaviour. What I see at the core of this whole business is abject human isolation surrounded by a floundering belief system.

I never regretted giving evidence against Greg. I did my duty, giving my testimony hard and exact. Once again, Tim helped me. When I showed him a copy of the statement I intended making to the police, he read it and said, 'Well, that's what you told me when you were 16.' That told me I wasn't imagining it. I didn't have to judge Greg and I didn't have to sentence him – for that I was grateful. Justice is an exhausting process and one part in that process was enough for me.

Outside the courtroom, I met the victim. I'd decided

long before to support him if ever asked. I had periodically thought of contacting him, but my experience as a journalist taught me that victims of sexual assaults do not always want to be reminded of what happened in the past, or be confronted with the possibility of other people in their families – like spouses and children – learning of it. We had a brief, awkward conversation. He was a working man with a working man's pride – conversation on this topic was beyond him. I walked away from the court, satisfied that justice had been done.

★

That day I also saw a copy of a letter dated 18 November 1971 from the rector of our school, Bernard Hosie, to Herman, then the order's provincial, concerning Greg's behaviour. Herman's signature, indicating receipt of the letter, was in the top left-hand corner.

I have regard for Bernard Hosie. Because of his teaching, I found that I was actually good at something, or rather two things – English and history. He'd seen action with the RAAF during the war and was clear about what he was and was not doing in the school. He didn't seek personal relations with the boys and wasn't very popular among them. It wasn't so much that I liked him; I learned from him. Within a few years, he would be out of the order and married.

This is the opening paragraph from his letter to Herman:

> I have reports of about 8 boys that Greg (they claim) has been fooling around with in his room. Some of them (3) saw 3 members of the Student Representative Council and told them. They at once saw me. It seems to have come to a head in the last week or two. Strange that Tom caught none of it though.

I'll take Hosie's letter point by point. I always thought it significant that when we fronted Hosie about Greg, he didn't contest our version of events. Here he says he has reports of 'about 8 boys'. That is, he had additional reports about Greg's behaviour to ours. I'd always assumed we were the only ones.

The full sentence reads: 'I have reports of about 8 boys that Greg (they claim) has been fooling around with in his room.' I have seen that phrase 'fooling around' used elsewhere to describe interactions of a sexual nature between clergy and boys around that time. The idea of what was going on being equated with foolishness smacks of euphemism. As a violation, the act whose aftermath I witnessed was in the vicinity of rape.

It's the last sentence of Hosie's opening paragraph that pulled me up. 'Strange that Tom caught none of it though.' If we define a paedophile as someone who draws a child into the realm of adult sexuality, Tom, by 1971, had been a practising paedophile for at least seven years. My reading is that Hosie didn't know that. Greg committed his sexual assault in 1971. Tom wasn't on the staff of the school in 1971 – he'd become the man lapping Australia trying to drum up recruits for the order (although I do recall him visiting our school that year). Why did Hosie expect Tom to have special knowledge in that area?

And now we arrive at what might be termed the play within the play. Suppose Tom did know. If Tom had told Hosie about Greg, he would have raised the spectre of paedophilia in the school. I'm guessing Tom would think that was not in his interests. Another question is, what did Greg know about Tom? I'm a great believer in the old saying, 'Get a thief to catch a thief.' Guilt can be detected at a glance by the guilty. Finally, the fact the letter is addressed to Herman as head of the order raises the drama to the level of a John le Carré novel: what did Herman know? I have no answers for any of these questions.

Hosie wrote, 'It seems to have come to a head in the last week or two.' That was my impression at the time, that Greg had walked ever closer to the line until in the end he well and truly fell over it. He'd built up from having kids in his room measuring the length of their cocks and wrestling on his bed to wrestling with a half-naked kid, pulling out his cock and ejaculating on him.

The substance of Hosie's letter is about what is to be

done with Greg. He favours keeping him around until the end of the year, then moving him interstate. Two of the other priests in the school say he should be moved on immediately. Hosie writes, 'The affair is pretty well known among the boys I fear … So if you had an urgent call for a man to go to a parish for a couple of weeks this might be wise.' Matriculation classes have ended for the year, and Hosie can get other priests to cover his teaching duties. 'It would therefore be very easy to move him if it had to be done overnight.'

Another plan is to withdraw Greg from all his classes and have him focus on the school magazine, *The Sword*. Student editor of *The Sword* that year? Martin 'Flaps' Flanagan, school vice-captain and 20th man in the worst First XVIII to represent the school in my six years. The coach, Roger, knew as much about football as I did about Euclidian geometry. His idea of a pre-match address was to buzz loudly.

Hosie finishes his letter with the words: 'I am, of course, frightened of a Court case. It would only need one parent to lay charges. We are sitting on a volcano, and it is not very pleasant.' He was sitting on a volcano alright, but it took another 43 years to blow.

★

Another document that has come into my hands is an investigator's report from the San Diego Police

Department dated December 2004. Bernard Hosie, married and living in La Jolla, California, is interviewed by reporting officer C. A. Gregg at the request of the Australian Federal Police about Greg and Roger. Hosie is described as 'very co-operative'. He is shown a copy of the November 1971 letter he wrote to Herman. C.A. Gregg writes:

> Mr Hosie said his recollection of that time period was vague, but he did remember there were allegations that [Greg] had been involved in some inappropriate activity with students. He also said that since he left the Order in the early '70s and emigrated to America from Australia, he had heard through unknown sources that [Roger] was possibly being investigated for the same type of activity. He said that he had always thought of [Greg] as a little 'wacky', but felt [Roger] was a fine, upright human being and did not believe the rumours about him.
>
> Mr Hosie said he had never been approached by any student who was victimised, or any parent, but rather had been appraised [sic] of the situation by members of the student council, although he could not remember details of that report ... Hosie said that he remembered some of the student board, whom he considered completely honest, had approached him with reports from some other students that [Greg] had been 'fooling around' with them ...

> Mr Hosie said he could not remember any specifics
> about the information brought to him by the student
> council. He is fairly certain he never talked to [Greg]
> directly about the charges because he would definitely
> remember that ...

I find it astonishing that Hosie never spoke to Greg 'directly about the charges'. Here were 12 men, committed to a religious vocation that made them responsible for the welfare of several hundred kids. One of their number commits a brazen sexual assault and the leader of the community doesn't talk to the offender, yet we know from Hosie's letter to Herman that he thought he was sitting on the edge of a volcano. Were the priests, ostensibly living in a fraternity, really that remote from one another? I have a friend who spent time as a novitiate in recent years who thinks so. He stated the unspoken rule of communal religious life, as he experienced it to be: 'Don't ask me how I'm coping with my demons, and I won't ask you how you're coping with yours.' Yet no doubt they still prayed together before each meal. This is a strange culture to me and, at some level, I come from it.

★

One day, maybe a week or two after we reported Greg to Hosie, I was on the senior oval with one of the boys

I'd made the report with. Greg was driving back from town in one of the school's three Holden sedans when, I surmise, he saw us. He parked next to the oval about 100 metres away, looking at us in a deeply moody sort of way. I sensed he was by now conscious of the terrible seriousness of his crime. He'd need to talk to someone, particularly if the other priests were giving him the silent treatment. I wonder to this day, had we gone over, what he would have said.

Perhaps because Dad was a school principal and I'd eavesdropped on enough of his business to know how he handled a crisis, how he stood at a distance, I said, 'Ignore him,' and we did. I knew it was a scandal, I knew it was out of our hands.

I didn't see Greg again until we went to court 30-odd years later. He looked like he'd been flattened like plants are in books; only he had been flattened by the weight of his crime. He stood pressed against the courtroom wall, eyes fixed at his feet, not once looking up.

★

It was Paul O'Halloran's lobbying that got the Royal Commission into Institutional Sexual Abuse to Tasmania. He also unearthed the case of 'Father GMG' in the Royal Commission report. Father GMG isn't named. He is sent to our school in 1966 after having been found guilty of some interaction of a sexual nature with a boy at his previous school in northern New South Wales while a dormitory master.

In October 1967, Father GMG advises the provincial of the order, a priest unknown to me, that his situation is 'grave'. He writes, 'I have had some serious temptations and I have decided I cannot in conscience allow myself to remain in circumstances which seem to produce these temptations – I mean of course, a boarding school, and especially care of a dormitory.'

The provincial responds by deciding to send him back to the school whence he has come. The rector of that school complains that there are boys at the school who know of Father GMG's previous 'problems', and that the situation with dormitory masters 'cannot be policed'. He suggests sending him to a school run by the order in southern New South Wales. 'At least boys can't get to his room there [and] there are no dormitories [and] day teachers have so little time with boys.'

So what did they do? They sent Father GMG to a psychiatrist. On 6 May 1968, the psychiatrist wrote 'the essence of the problem is that this person had a homosexual problem which over recent years has diminished considerably to the extent that he is now fairly well heterosexually inclined … I suggested I see him several more times to give him some little psychotherapy to help him get out of some of his difficulties.'

Really? How exactly do you 'diminish' a homosexual orientation to the extent that the patient is 'fairly well heterosexually inclined'? What does 'fairly well hetero-sexually inclined' mean, anyway? What does 'some little psychotherapy' entail? What evidence was there that the 'little psychotherapy' exercises did indeed 'help him get out of some of his difficulties'? The psychiatrist with his glib affirmations was one of many external players who have a responsibility for what happened at places like my old school.

★

I look back in time and see an image from those years. Father GMG is taking showers. Surrounded by lots of hot pink flesh, from boys to naked young men with athletic bodies. He's leaning back against a hand basin, head down, hand to his face, eyes closed. I see a man trying not to look. I see a man fighting 'serious temp-tation'. One who knows his situation is 'grave'. Could someone fighting his personal battle be put in a more desperate situation?

The most charitable interpretation of the decision to place him there is that it was the action of someone with no knowledge of the world whatsoever. Was it wilful ignorance? I don't think wilful ignorance is rare. I think it's a daily practice – like the wilful ignorance we exercise in relation to issues like off-shore detention.

About Father GMG, the report of the Royal Commission continues: 'Between 1972 and 1981, Father

GMG returned to the same school in northern New South Wales where he was appointed a classroom teacher and dormitory discipline master and also to a senior position at the school. One person made a claim in 2014 that he was sexually abused by Father GMG in the late 1970s.

'In the 1980s and early 1990s, Father GMG was appointed to various positions, including a senior position at the school in Tasmania, working in parishes in Victoria, and again as a teacher and dormitory master at the same school in northern New South Wales in 1988 and 1992. Between 1993 and 1994, he was appointed chaplain of a Catholic school, run by an order of brothers, in Sydney.

'Following an anonymous phone call to the Order in 1993 in relation to allegations of sexual abuse, Father GMG acknowledged that there may be grounds for the laying of criminal charges against him relating to an incident at the school in northern New South Wales in 1976. Father GMG was withdrawn from his position at the Catholic school in Sydney and placed on a restricted ministry in 1993.'

That phrase – 'a restricted ministry' – could be the (deeply ironic) title of a book.

★

John Girdauskas is a man of medium height with a slow smile and a self-effacing manner which comes with a certain weariness. His father was a refugee from Lithuania, his mother a Dutch immigrant. (The difference? One had difficulty getting into Australia, the other didn't.) He grew up in the town where the old school stands and is now its parish priest. In 2019, he did a story with journalist Henry Zwartz and ABC Tasmania in which he said he was sexually abused by a priest while a student at the school.

Girdauskas has the flat, frank manner of a man who has gone beyond pretending. He tells me from the get-go that he's gay. As a kid at the old school, he was 'terribly lonely'. The family had little money, he wasn't into sport. He was 'drawn to the person of Jesus' and enjoyed being an altar boy. That's how, in 1968 when he was 14, he met a priest I'll call Laurie (his first name). Laurie died in 1993 and was never charged, but he is the subject of other allegations which suggest a consistent modus operandi.

I asked him to describe Laurie who had been a missionary in Japan. 'He was likable but strange. Odd. There was something about his oddness some kids liked. Sometimes, he'd say the Mass in Japanese. I'd have no idea what was going on.'. Laurie often said the Mass in Latin. His was a highly formal Catholicism. He didn't like priests who dressed casually – he'd say they didn't look like 'a proper priest'.

Laurie took 14-year-old John to a remote rural presbytery, and left him sitting in a room. Laurie then reappeared naked sporting a giant erection, urging John to take off his clothes and do the same. Laurie cooked food and ate at the table naked with his giant erection. Later, he encouraged John to masturbate and masturbated while watching.

I asked John if Laurie expressed tenderness or love during their sexual encounters. 'He did, but afterwards he was distant from you like he had the shits, like you'd done something wrong.'

Girdauskas went to Laurie when Laurie was hearing confession and confessed about what they had done together. From the other side of the confessional box, he heard Laurie say, 'I can't forgive you because I've been complicit.' Their sexual relationship lasted four years. After each encounter, as he dropped John back at his parents' place, Laurie would say, 'What happened is between you and me. Don't worry about it.'

He remembers odd things about Laurie. He was into killing snakes. When bushwalking, he always carried a stick for that purpose. Laurie said of his father, 'Daddy was very prudish.' Laurie prided himself on not being prudish. He would take John on bush walks and, finding a place with water, he'd strip off naked with the pretence of sunning himself even when there was no sun. He'd talk or make jokes of a sexual nature. Once, camping in a small tent, Laurie complained how hot it was, unzipped his sleeping bag, and then proceeded to openly masturbate, wanting John to do the same.

The youth felt trapped. Laurie was friends with his parents.

It was a relief for Girdauskas to learn many years later that Laurie had other victims. One of the questions he had always asked himself was, 'Why me? Why was I the special one?' He realises now that Laurie 'was adept at picking out boys who were a bit different. He took advantage of the fact that I had shown an interest in a vocation to the priesthood, and I believe he saw this as an opportunity to firm up an association with me to get his rocks off.'

There's an earthiness about John Girdauskas that might surprise some in a priest. He swears because he favours direct means of expression. He says his parents were earthy too, and didn't push him towards the priesthood. As a kid, he looked up to some of the priests he knew. There are still priests he looks up to. 'I'm sure they've had their trials. But they're kind men.' His nickname at school, and in the seminary, was Johnny G.

He was always 'a bit rebellious'. He once attended a meeting where a bishop declared, 'Homosexuals are not part of God's plan.' Girdauskas replied, 'I am a gay man and, as far as I'm concerned, I am part of God's plan and God loves me.' He still loves the gospel message.

He explains his theology with a series of phrases with pauses between them. 'God, He or She, is the enabler of people to lead fuller lives ... none of us are perfect ... Jesus is the one who inspires, he's the voice … fundamentally, when we die, we're not going to be asked how many times we went to church, we're going to be asked how we have loved … most people are good people … we're all in that boat together.'

When I asked John Girdauskas why he became a priest, I added, 'I imagine everyone asks you that.' He smiled and said, 'They do.' His answer was relatively simple. 'There were some priests I liked. There was something these men did that I was attuned to. I was young and idealistic, I wanted to be one of those priests that help people.' He joined Laurie's order, the order that ran the school. 'There was something warm and welcoming about them as a group of men.' He mentions Brother Jim, the old bloke who drove the tractor round the school and had spent his early life working with horses. Brother Jim had a peasant's faith that was large and generous. (He signed the papers which allowed the Hobart gang to buy the Simca Aronde.)

We talked mutual acquaintances and I asked about a priest called Moynihan. He came to the school late in my time, a little bloke with a broken nose who'd played for one of the big Sydney rugby league clubs like Saint George. I didn't have much to do with him but one night we had a long conversation and I saw what he was on about. Seems he spent the rest of his life living in shared houses with homeless and Indigenous people. He was a humble, working-class bloke with a generous vision. I also mentioned a priest from the school for whom I have a continuing dislike. 'He was cruel,' said John. That's what I thought. A remorseless bully with words, aiming to wound and, in my case, succeeding.

Girdauskas says of the conservative faction in Catholic hierarchy, 'With them, there's no listening to other voices. There's a significant number of people who want a new way. If there is any future for the Church, they will have to embrace the reality of the human condition, of life as it is, and be far more embracing of diversity. I was of the belief that I could make a difference if I reached out to people. I love people, I love the diversity of life, I'm not scared of that. I'm a gay man who was the son of a refugee. I long for a more welcoming church.' He said the fate of whistleblowers about sexual abuse in the Catholic Church is loneliness and isolation. 'You're a problem. Go away.'

★

I concur with John Girdauskas's judgement of the priests of our shared era – a lot, he says, were people 'who hadn't grown in their psychosexual development. They were boys really and suddenly they were confronted by humanity as it really is. They were fellows who hardly knew who they were, and they were sent to run this boarding school. The Church accepted these young men who had no experience of life, no knowledge of their own sexuality, hetero or homo, and placed them in a situation where ... they had control.' That's what I like about John Girdauskas. He knows who he is. He's real.

Girdauskas was in the order from 1975 until 1998 when he left, having become disillusioned with 'living in community'. The rot set in when he shared a house in Queensland with, of all people, Tom and Greg. Greg was the boss. John describes him as 'scatty'. Greg decided to close a primary school in the parish. The locals objected, but Greg claimed he had the bishop's support – a letter from the bishop was found stating the opposite. Chaos ensued. We had a few laughs about Greg. Like the way he'd make big pronouncements from the pulpit on local issues that then found their way into the local newspaper. Once he made a big statement about drugs in the region and the drug squad visited the school to ask why Greg knew more about drugs in the area than they did. As for Tom, when he had a few drinks, all he could talk about was sex.

In 1998, Girdauskas took leave of the order, went to live in West Australia, had nothing to do with the Church, didn't even go to Mass, and worked as a carer 'cleaning bottoms'. In 2000, he became a priest again, but not as a member of any religious order – as an ordinary priest in a diocese answerable to the archbishop. Coming back to Tasmania brought back the memory of his abuse. Then he was sent to the town where the old school was.

It was when Paul and Steve O'Halloran came out

publicly that Girdauskas thought, 'I need to deal with this. I want an apology from these blokes.' He wrote a letter to the provincial. In his reply, the provincial said he neither believed nor disbelieved him, but as Laurie was dead it was not a matter he could comment further on. The schism between Girdauskas and the order remains. John Girdauskas says his despair is that the whole matter will never end. He wants to forgive Laurie, but can't.

As the local parish priest, Girdauskas had also observed the continuing consequences of the various priests' sexual misbehaviour. 'The community was hurting. There was a sense of sadness, of shame. In a small place like this, lots of people know a survivor. It has a ripple effect of heartache and disbelief and anger.' There was also the contrary problem – people in the community who didn't believe any of it had occurred.

He rang an associate of the archbishop and asked 'where the hell' the archbishop was. 'Our community is hurting. There are no phone calls. He needs to come to our parish and be the shepherd. He needs to be here.' A nervous archbishop came. 'I said, "They're not going to bash you up. They just want you to listen."' A group of 30 gathered, and at that meeting, in the presence of the Archbishop of Tasmania, John Girdauskas revealed that he had been abused by Laurie. 'I was emotional, I was teary. I said we needed a public acknowledgment in a structured way.' The archbishop agreed. This was the origin of the Ritual of Lament.

★

The classic exposition of boarding-school life is George Orwell's essay 'Such, Such Were the Joys'. (It was written, I read once, just before he started work on *Nineteen Eighty-Four*. No surprises there.) Brave as always, Orwell begins, 'Soon after I arrived at St Cyprian's … I began wetting my bed.' He is, at the time, all of eight years old. The first quarter of the essay details the school's response to his bed-wetting.

The boarding school is run by a husband and wife known to the kids as Sambo and Flip. Orwell provides vivid portraits of both, particularly Flip, with her 'deep-set, suspicious eyes', the way she has favourites and the manner in which she dispenses her favours. Orwell is beaten by Sambo for wetting the bed. 'He had already taken a bone-handled riding-crop out of the cupboard, but it was part of the punishment of reporting yourself that you had to proclaim your offence with your own lips.' That's the shit I hate. Being made complicit in your own pain.

Young Orwell is overheard by Flip telling another kid the beating hadn't hurt him and is dragged back in. 'This time Sambo laid on in real earnest. He continued for a length of time that frightened and astonished me – about five minutes, it seemed – ending up by breaking the riding-crop … "Look what you've made me do!" he said furiously, holding the broken crop. I had fallen into a chair, weakly snivelling.'

This is his equivalent of me in Herman's office begging for mercy. Orwell describes 'a sense of desolate loneliness and helplessness'. That's me in third year.

'To grasp the effect of this kind of thing on a child of 10 or 12, one has to remember that the child … will accept what it is told, and it will believe in the most fantastic way in the knowledge and powers of the adults surrounding it.'

Here I beg to differ. I'm not pretending I was a dissident at 10 or 12, but I didn't believe 'in the most fantastic way' in the knowledge and powers of the adults around me. I watched out for the priests like pedestrians at zebra crossings watch out for cars. In my critical year, the third, when I was 13, it wasn't the adults who put terror into my heart, it was the boys.

★

Any full appreciation of what went on in places like my old school has to take into account what the boys did to the boys. It's not about laying blame. It's about having a real idea of what those places were like.

To make my point another way: if a *Lord of the Flies* scenario happened today – that is, a planeload of British schoolboys went missing – the media would be buzzing with speculation about the pilot's mental health, the standards of the operating airline etc. There would be footage of weeping families. The boys would be assumed – that is, they would be *portrayed* as – innocents. They are innocent in the sense that they have played no part in creating the situation they are trapped in. But it doesn't follow that their behaviour within that situation is innocent.

I once read that *Lord of the Flies* had its genesis in Golding and his wife visiting a cathedral where a boys' choir was singing. Watching the choir in full and glorious voice, Golding's wife sighed, 'They're angels,' to which Golding replied, 'That's what you think.' Jack, the king bully in *Lord of the Flies*, leads his young followers to murder, but when he first lands on the island he's a choirboy. It's on this basis that he claims leadership of the group when it is debated early in the book. 'I ought to be chief because I'm chapter chorister and head boy ... I can sing C sharp.' It's one of the best lines in the book.

★

How different was my boarding school to other boarding schools? An old boy of one of Victoria's elite Protestant private schools who read this manuscript described its contents as 'familiar'. He wrote, 'I knew the bullies, I knew the teachers, I too retreated into sport.' I asked an acquaintance who was sent off to one of Tasmania's foremost Protestant boarding schools at the age of seven the worst thing about his experience. He replied, 'Being bullied … and becoming a bully.'

My oldest friend is a woman born in the same hospital a day before me. As a boarder at a Protestant girls' school, she found herself surrounded by tormentors in one of those hellish circles I described at the start of the book. A friend of hers broke through the circle and pulled her out. I know the friend, a Tasmanian farm girl of independent mind and character. I always liked her but hearing how she rescued my friend has placed her in my personal Hall of Fame (I'm talking about you, MS!).

I am a collector of boarding school anecdotes and literature. For example, my old school was a romp in the park compared to Harrow in the early 19th century. I learned about it reading a biography of the poet Lord Byron by Benita Eisler. In 1801, when he arrived as a 13-year-old boarder, Harrow, one of the pillars of the British establishment, basically had the same sexual mores as American prisons today. As Eisler puts it, 'In Harrow's homoerotic underworld, every form of transgressive sexuality, from gang rape to sadomasochistic activity, was openly indulged.'

Eisler quotes from a manuscript deposited in the London Library by a Harrow old boy named A. J. Symonds, who attended the school in the 1850s: 'Every boy of good looks had a female name and was recognized either as a public prostitute or as some bigger fellow's bitch.' There is a letter from Byron's schooldays in which he offers his 'protection' to a younger boy with whom he had fallen in love because of his beautiful singing voice.

In that context, here is a line from *Tom Brown's School Days*, written by Thomas Hughes as a homage to the Rugby school in England and published in 1857: 'He was one of those miserable little pretty white-handed, curly-haired boys, petted and pampered by some of the big fellows, who wrote their verses for them, taught them to drink and use bad language, and did all they could to spoil them for everything in this world and the next.'

★

Tom Brown, of *Tom Brown's School Days*, is the great boarding-school hero – he fights a bully to protect a smaller boy called Arthur, although the point needs to be made that Arthur was in the same house as Tom (by name, School House). The various houses at Rugby were like competing infant nations – when they played Rugby football against one another (at this time the game was played nowhere but Rugby), they wore jerseys bearing the crests of the great European nations so that, for example, France played Prussia. It was a war game.

This is from the chapter of *Tom Brown's School Days*

dedicated to the fight: 'Let those young persons whose stomachs are not strong, or who consider a good set-to with the weapons God has given us all uncivilized, unchristian, or ungentlemanly affair, just skip this chapter, because it won't be to their taste … fighting with fists is the natural and English way for English boys to settle their quarrels.'

The fight he describes is longer, more arduous and more dangerous than any I witnessed. It is also more organised. The boys fight stripped to the waist in the manner of London prize-fighters. There are a time-keeper and seconds – a friend lends a knee to serve as a stool for the fighter between rounds while his face is sponged. Wagers are made on the outcome. Tom is aged 13, maybe 14. My school is half a planet and 130 years away but I can visualise exactly what is being depicted. However numerous the differences between my old school and Rugby in the 1830s, what is overwhelmingly the same is the reality of living in a juvenile culture.

Tom Brown's fight gets to the fifth round and is still undecided. Both are bloodied. Tom is smaller and younger than the bully, Slogger Williams, but also fitter and quicker. Both fighters have hurt and been hurt. Slogger 'hopes to finish it with some heavy right-handed blow'. If you know anything about boxing, you know exactly what punch he aims to deliver. Both are fatigued. Tom is waiting for Slogger to drop his guard to get in and land telling blows. The cock of the school, a boy in 'the Sixth', sees what's going on but lets them fight, believing it's for the best.

The character I identify with is Arthur, the small boy with whom the dispute between Tom and Slogger Williams began. Arthur now undergoes a crisis. The fight has been going for more than 30 minutes, there seems to be no end to it. In Arthur's head he's hearing stories of London prize-fighters who have died in the ring. He is witnessing something abhorrent to his nature – if he acts to stop it by informing the school authorities, he is violating the boys' culture which forbids dobbing. He either betrays himself or he betrays the juvenile culture to which he belongs.

★

I have a confession to make. I was troubled by the Great Food Walk-Out of 1968. Tim had told me beforehand what was going to happen. He was for the walk-out, so I was too – but I seemed to know it was a revolutionary act and there would be all sorts of consequences.

I think now that I must have always felt a bit sorry for the priests. Theirs was such a poor existence. They lived in their little rooms, they had only a handful of clothes (we knew because we saw them being recycled). They performed their duties for no pay, their food wasn't a whole lot better than ours and they did it for – us. I never hated them. I just didn't understand them. They were strange to me. A particularly gentle one I recall was like a moth who lived in a missal. He wandered round murmuring prayers and spoke with a lisp. His nickname was Lipth.

I am in awe of what Peter Rowe did, leading the walk-out. It was a peasants' revolt, a group of people who had no political power claiming some. I remember seeing him rise from his chair when the day's swill arrived and say something to the effect of 'We're out', and a crowd of kids rose from their chairs and headed for the door of the refectory. The priest in charge that day, poor old Lipth, waved his hands ineffectually, but it was like trying to stop a rush-hour crowd at Flinders Street station.

Maybe it was the power of Eric's oratory that evening, when he hissed with rage and said if he knew which boys had organised the walk-out he'd punch their teeth into the pit of their bellies. Sixty boys blanched as one, but as always with Eric when he went off the charts with anger and then performed the immense feat of holding the red force in, I felt his hurt. Later that night I saw Bernard Hosie – there was disappointment in his face. I apologised for walking out, and said the junior boys (of whom I was one) hadn't led it. He replied, 'I know that, Flanagan,' and kept walking. That left me feeling worse. I'd dobbed. Why? And for what? I was catapulted into an agony of doubt. More confusion.

A lot of years later, I read where the Swiss psychologist Carl Jung said anyone 'who attempts to both adjust to his group and at the same time pursue his individual goal, becomes neurotic'. I guess that's you and me, Arthur.

*

The fight between Tom Brown and Slogger Williams goes to a sixth round. Arthur snaps, running and telling the school matron, who hurries off and informs the headmaster. His arrival at the scene disperses the boys. Tom is left, in the author's view, none the worse. He has 'a slight difficulty in his vision, a singing in his ears, and a sprained thumb'. A boy is dispatched to the local butcher to buy a raw steak to stop Tom's eye swelling. And that is how Arthur finds Tom, holding a steak to his eye.

Desperate for the violence to stop, Arthur says to Tom, 'You won't go on, will you? You'll promise me you won't go on?' Tom laughingly replies, 'Can't tell about that – all depends on the houses. We're in the hands of our countrymen, you know. Must fight for the school-flag, if so be.' And so the moral of the best-read and most influential English-language schoolboy tale of the 19th century is that the hero will fight for his country if his country asks and it is in the interests of the country's flag. From such beliefs empires are made.

That night Tom is woken and invited to the

sixth-form room where a council of senior boys awaits him. Welcomed into their midst, he is commended for his pluck, given bottled beer to drink and a seat at their table, 'one of that much-envied society'. He's told to make it up with Slogger Williams, which he does next morning, and they become great mates. In tribal terms, he's been initiated.

★

The Indigenous brother who smoked me to protect me from literary critics also took me to his people's initiation place near the Murray River. A giant slab of rock sliding down a hill had created a cave where the ceremony had been conducted, presumably for thousands of years. The brother approached the place with awe. His clan no longer practised formal initiation rites, but he thought that was preferable to having individuals without the proper cultural authority and knowledge conducting initiations which, he said, was happening.

More than once in northern Australia, I encountered the Aboriginal idea that there's two ways of doing things – 'proper way' and 'wrong way'. 'Initiations can be done wrong way,' he said. 'I know,' I replied, 'My initiation was done wrong way.' He got what I meant, knowing people who had grown up in institutions.

★

And now, my all-time favourite boarding-school story. The star of this story is Yawuru man Patrick Dodson, rightly called the father of the Australian reconciliation movement. The great influence on Patrick's early life was his grandfather, a 'senior' man in what Aboriginal people call 'the Law', who also identified as a Catholic. It was his grandfather who told Patrick there was nothing in the Jesus story that was incompatible with the Law.

In his 13th year, Patrick was growing up near Katherine in the Northern Territory, wanting to be an Aboriginal cowboy like the other young Aboriginal men he knew. Aboriginal stockmen were hard proud men, like Argentinian gauchos. Patrick had all the necessary attributes. I once went fishing with him and his nephew, a local football coach with a pit bull terrier tattooed on his right bicep, in Broome's Roebuck Bay. All of a sudden, the nephew's rod bent almost into a circle and we started being towed around the bay by what turned out to be a three-metre hammerhead shark.

Sweating profusely, Patrick and his nephew pulled the beast in, the battle lasting about an hour. When they finally got the furious creature up beside the boat, Patrick moved over and leant across to grab it – with one last frenzied shake of its hideous head, it snapped the line and swam off, circling the boat.

Later, over a beer, I said to Patrick, 'You can't have

been serious about wrestling that shark into the boat.' He assured me he was, showing me the headlock traditionally employed for the exercise. 'Elbows in when wrestling sharks,' he advised.

When Patrick was 13, both his parents died within a couple of months. His older sister and a local priest decided to send him as a boarder to Monivae College in faraway Hamilton, western Victoria. Being Aboriginal, Patrick Dodson was not at this time counted as a human being in the national census. Within four years, he was school captain, captain of the First XVIII and adjutant of the school cadets corps. He'd also acted to eliminate bullying.

After leaving Monivae, Patrick became a priest and was sent to a traditional Aboriginal community in the Northern Territory. He encouraged the people to continue with their ceremonies – their men's and women's business – telling them that their blackfella ceremonies were what the Catholic Church called sacraments. Hearing of this, the Bishop of Darwin, an Irishman, accused him of paganism. Patrick parted company with the Church. Nonetheless he remains a compellingly unique figure in Australian public life, one who is fluent in the western intellectual tradition while also, as an initiated man, having traditional Aboriginal knowledge.

Once when I was with Patrick in the Kimberley, the subject of boarding schools arose. I said it was the bullying that got to me, and he casually remarked, 'We managed to cut that out at Monivae.' Intrigued, I led him further into the subject. He related how one day he came across a big boy holding a little boy out a window by his ankles on the second floor of a building. 'I said, "Bring him in, mate."' He smiled at the memory and said no more, but I knew what happened. The bully brought the little boy in. When genuinely tough people talk to you in a polite but definite manner, if you're half-smart you listen.

Patrick's campaign to eliminate bullying came down to one big fight. He said no more beyond naming his adversary. He smiled at that memory too and I gathered the bout was decided in his favour. About 10 years later, I met the bloke he fought, a big muscular man, a rural conservative. He was so proud of having Patrick as his friend.

The biggest fight of my journalistic career was over a story I wrote about Patrick which was altered by an editor. I won, and the story appeared exactly as I wrote it. The next time I saw Patrick I said, 'You know that story I wrote on you – it was quite a fight.' He replied with a pointed single word, 'Yes.' I realised conveying Aboriginal reality was a battle he fought every day and here I was congratulating myself for fighting it once. For the record, I believe Patrick Dodson is one of the great Australians, if not the great Australian, of my generation.

Just as this book was being finished, I happened to run into former *Age* colleague Tony Wright, a seasoned and gifted observer of the human condition who happened to be at Monivae with Patrick. His memory was jolted by the story about the big kid holding the little kid out the window by his ankles. He said, 'I know something about that.' We talked about the fight that decided the matter and he said in an animated way, 'Patrick was strong emotionally and mentally, but he was also strong physically. You didn't fool with him. Patrick Dodson's word was law at Monivae.'

In 1960s Australia, a black kid transformed a white boarding school from within. Tell me that wouldn't make a great Australian movie! *Rabbit-Proof Fence* meets *To Sir with Love*.

★

When I needed friends, when I was 13, I didn't have any. Not really. I do not in the least blame any of my contemporaries for that. Most wouldn't have known what was going on. Some made a choice not to know, but I don't blame them for that either, because I made the same choice the night I saw the kid in the next bed weeping and did nothing. To be frank, when I left school and no longer needed male friends, I silently rejoiced. But once I stopped needing friends in a desperate way, I started collecting them in a free and easy way.

My university years were a lot of fun. My girlfriend and I were seldom apart. I did a law degree that taught me valuable lessons that benefited me as a journalist, the biggest being that if your work is being scrutinised by trained minds, you won't get away with bullshit.

I joined the Tasmanian University Football Club, arriving at the age of 17 years and one month, eager, impressionable and up for a good time. I had hair down to my arse and used to run laps barefooted because I got energy from the earth. The first night at training we were called into the centre of the ground by senior coach Brian 'Cocky' Eade. Spying me and my bare feet on the edge of the circle, he cried out, 'What the fuck have I got here?!'

I became the club bard and, while not much of a player, was appointed captain-coach of the Fourth XVIII. I think my gift was bringing people together and creating team spirit. We're born alone and we die alone, and along the way we get a few opportunities to make lasting bonds with other people – playing footy was one of them. I wanted my players to have a good time, and winning made the good times better. My approach seemed to work. I was subsequently made coach of the Thirds and then the Seconds.

Paul O'Halloran played in a Thirds team of mine that made a memorable grand final. I had spent the whole week wrestling with fear – fortunately, my fear of getting hit was overcome by my fear of playing badly when I was the captain-coach and I played okay. After the match, the competition hard man, who played for a working-class club that was hostile to university students (this being the era of the Vietnam War), flung open the steel door of our change rooms, marched through the crowd to where I sat and landed beside me, handing me a beer to go with the one in his hand in a gesture of public respect. That was the highlight of my footy career. I never played again.

That same year, I found myself in a drinking circle with three fellas from the old school, Paul O'Halloran one of them. Someone mentioned the school and one of them blurted, 'Tom got me.' 'And me,' said Paul. 'And me,' said the third. But not me. It was another of those curious moments when you are both intimately connected and completely apart. But I did wonder if more had gone on at the old school than I knew.

There was another occasion I never forgot, when I snuck into a Hobart pub as a 16-year-old and found a very drunk former head prefect leaning against the bar. He hardly seemed to recognise me but mumbled something about the school being a factory for paedophiles. I didn't quite believe him, but I never forgot the exchange.

Maybe I should have thought more about it at the time, but I didn't. I'd left the Catholic Church without a backward glance. I was never going back, not to the Church, not to the school. I avoided people I'd been to school with. How could you talk about what we'd been through? People don't understand how deeply personal the experience was, how incredibly different the various versions of what occurred can be.

What if I open up to you and you don't believe me? What if you open up to me and I don't believe you? Even if we agree on the facts – or some of them – our interpretation could be as far apart as fire from water, as laughter from tears. It's all too hard when there are simple responses like being polite and keeping your distance.

*

Early 2020, I met Rinso at Tim's. It was like meeting the platoon commander you went through a war with. He's done well in life, lives in a rich part of Sydney. I told him about this manuscript and asked him if he'd read it. He said he would but didn't look enthusiastic. I was a few weeks awaiting a response during which time I got mildly nervous. What if he objected to what I'd written? Then I received an email saying he had put off reading it, fearing it contained confronting material. He'd been pleasantly surprised by what he read, surprised also that he had received a few mentions. We arranged to speak on the phone.

That was a long conversation. Rinso had read the book in the way that some people, buying houses, become intimate with all aspects of the building's construction and appearance. He'd listed the typos. I said the typos were the last thing I worried about, but he did not easily leave the subject. I sensed the power of a mind not easily swayed.

He asked me questions about different people in the book. Told me a story about Smithie, the kid from the Bass Strait island who was different. A group of kids had been taken swimming at a beach and Smithie had come out of the water stark naked. A startled priest had ordered the other kids, Rinso among them, to hurriedly circle Smithie so that he would be hidden from public view.

Rinso tells his stories well. Not one word more than necessary. I can see his stories like I'm watching them in a cinema. After he left school, he was called up into the army. This was the time of the Vietnam War. Some of the blokes had trouble with military life – Rinso thought boarding school helped him in this regard.

Rinso brought up the matter of his bashing. This is where things got really interesting for me. Once-in-a-lifetime interesting. Seeing Rinso get bashed gutted me. I was 11 but I understood with a dull terrible certainty that I was watching an alternative view of human history, one where good people, men and women, get hammered into submission.

I remember the bully having one companion, Rinso says two – but I recall he was the smallest. I was at the other end of an empty corridor and too far away to hear what was being said but I knew Rinso was refusing to surrender ground. Suddenly the bully's hands leapt out in a sequence of punches. Rinso had a flood of blood down his front – he bled so much he found blood in his underpants that night. One of his tear ducts was split. He responded gamely but was just too small. For over 50 years, that image has been one of despair for me.

So what does Rinso tell me? He tells me he thinks he won the fight. I can't believe my ears.

He says, 'Even at the time I was thinking he doesn't have to do this. He doesn't have to beat someone who's so small, who has no defence. He's humiliating himself. I knew he'd lose out in the long term. He actually gave me strength.'

Rinso has something else to say.

'Reading your manuscript made me think about you.' I brace myself – judgement day has arrived. 'What I remember about you is your smile. You were friendly. There were people in that place who weren't.'

★

Two bouts of cancer have made my brother Tim reflect on what he chooses to invest his remaining life energy in. It amounts to a philosophy of health. Inspired by Rinso, Tim started contacting fellas he'd gone to school with. One evening, as he and I were walking around the edge of Great Oyster Bay, he started talking about the people he'd contacted. The sea was slowly slapping the sand beside us and when we left the beach to take a track through the coastal gums, the half-light made everything more dramatic. 'They're such nice, quiet blokes,' he said. 'That was the tragedy of the place.'

He told me he was organising a lunch for them in a country pub. I said I'd go. It would be the first old boys function I'd ever attended. Among the kids from my time that I knew, there had never been any move whatsoever to meet until Rinso showed up. It was like we shared a past nobody wanted to revisit. Rinso didn't see it like that. In his unwaveringly straightforward and cheerful way, he enjoyed meeting up and assumed others would also.

A dozen came to that first lunch. And so it was that we were together again, like members of a long-lost family who had finally reunited. A couple I had known at university, most I had seen only once or twice. Not only was it the first time we'd met since leaving school, it was, no less significantly, the first time we'd met since the avalanche of bad news had descended on the old school.

How would I describe that day?

Gentle. Remarkably gentle. It was like a group of people meeting in the wake of an invisible explosion – no-one's sure what really happened, who's hurt or how much or where. Everyone seemed to accept that something had happened, but what? All present, it seemed to me, had embarked on the journey of re-examining their memories, of replaying the old film clips of those times in their heads.

★

I sat next to Don Tracey, a jovial man with deep brown eyes. At school, he was a country kid, good at sport, known as 'Sticks' for his skinny legs. I'd liked him. We met once in 1987. I was at the MCG covering a game between Melbourne and the Swans. I went for a piss and was leaving the toilet when a man sped past, grabbed my hand, shook it, said, 'Don Tracey,' and hurried off with a backwards wave. It had always left me wondering. Now I learned his first wife died when she was 33 of breast cancer. That was their last trip to Melbourne, their last visit to the MCG, he was rushing back to her in the stands. The story is so powerful it rushes through my head like a technicolour movie.

Late in the day, the conversation moved to the school's four houses. I went round my end of the table, telling each person which house he was in. One fella couldn't remember the name of any of the school's four houses. I told him he was in Xavier house and wore number 13 in the senior football team. One of them said, 'How do you remember stuff like that?', and I said, 'Some things I remember.' I told Don Tracey he was in

Loyola. 'The yellow ones,' he said. Yes. Saint Ignatius Loyola played in yellow.

Rodney Oborne was there. He's my first footy vision – a blue flash cutting sideways through a pack in the Under 13s. Lithe, balanced, ahead of the game in thought and deed. He kicked 39 goals for Collingwood from a forward flank as a 19-year-old. Finished as an attacking defender in Tommy Hafey's great doomed Collingwood sides of the late 1970s, a role which required a stronger build than the one he actually possessed. Walks now with two bent knees from football injuries, my nomination for the Tasmanian AFL Hall of Fame.

Kev O'Dea was there. If you wanted to create the stereotype of a kid who was going to be bullied at my old school, it would be Kev O'Dea. He had a disability that affected both his speech and physical movements. One of the place's worst insults was spastic and I know he copped it. I ask Kev if he got bullied at our school. 'Not really,' he says and smiles. Kev's smile never leaves him. It never did back then. He's a follower of Indian guru Sathya Sai Baba and a keen Swans fan. It mattered a lot that Kev was there.

There was only goodwill at the table.

★

Newie was there. Real name Tony Newport. Solid as the mountains he grew up among. There's something, some public approbation, most people need that Newie doesn't, and in that way he reminds me of my father. A thinker, he never wastes a word, not in conversation nor in his letters to newspapers.

Newie's from Rosebery, the isolated West Coast mining town where we lived from 1964 to '68. We just passed through – he was born there and is a product of the place. His working-class mother and grandmother paid to send him to boarding school, his mother working a second job cleaning floors. Newie had two uncles with intellectual disabilities who lived with his grandmother and had a place in that community. His letters to newspapers are usually about community.

He's been a bank teller, miner, trade unionist, mediator, busker. I didn't know him well at school – he's a few years older – but meeting again half a century later we found we have many beliefs in common. One is that people's stories, truly told, are sacrosanct. Newie's the person I end up going to the Ritual of Lament with.

★

In my 40s, I met Graeme 'Gypsy' Lee, captain coach of East Devonport's 1968 premiership team, and was delighted to find he was the man I thought he was when I was an alienated 13-year-old. We became close – with Gypsy, there was so much I didn't have to say. He asked me to speak at his funeral and said he'd kick the lid of the coffin if I talked too long. He died in April 2021 and it was my honour to deliver his eulogy.

Gypsy was a descendant of Tasmanian Aboriginal chief Mannalargenna, seer and warrior of repute. Mannalargenna could make things happen. Gypsy made something happen, and I was there to witness it. Gypsy took my sense of sport as theatre to a whole other level, a place where fantastic stories can come true before your eyes.

In 1968, when I first encountered Gypsy, I didn't have a relationship with an adult male. I respected my father but didn't really know him. My relationship with the other men in my life – the priests – was confused and confusing. What Gypsy represented was simple and brilliantly, undeniably real. I would have played my heart out for Gypsy and by the end of his life he would have played his heart out for me. What I said at his funeral was thank you.

★

Gilroye Griffin III is an African-American eccentric with whom I exchange views on Australian football, politics and literature. I sent him this manuscript which he read, as did his wife Arlene, a Filipina American Catholic. Arlene, who is strong and smart, wrote, 'I respect that you wrote without judgement of those who still believed in the faith. I too make the clear distinction of those who are faithful and church as the institution.'

Gilroye was taken with the references to *Lord of the Flies* because he was teaching the book to a class of 14-year-olds in San Francisco. He asked me to do a Zoom session with his kids.

When I read the book, in 1969, I was the age the kids I was going to talk to were. American author Stephen King wrote of his adolescent response to *Lord of the Flies*: 'It was, so far as I can remember, the first book with hands – strong ones that reached out of the pages and seized me by the throat.' It was the first novel that transported me to an imaginary world that seemed as real as the one I inhabited.

Gilroye wanted me to talk about my relationship with the book so I started by quoting an exchange soon after the plane crash, where one of the kids says, 'Aren't there are any grown-ups on the island at all?' Piggy, the intellectual, says, 'I don't think so.' Can you imagine that degree of loneliness? The sense that a whole layer of human intelligence is missing? The island I lived on for six years had grown-ups, but they were not of us.

I didn't get the book totally when I was 14. I didn't get Simon's delirious conversation with the buzzing head of the dead pig. That's what the *Lord of the Flies* is – a dead pig's head impaled on a stick. It's the symbol of the group, a symbol of its new-found power, one which enables them to do evil. Therefore, the logic runs, the pig's head is evil. Simon tells the pig's head it's only a pig's head.

Evil is a word I was never comfortable with, not knowing what it really means. However, in the early 2000s, when I was confronted with the issue of torture in South Africa, evil was the word – the plain, simple word – that immediately came to mind. I will attempt a definition: evil is accumulated bad behaviour that acquires a personality and will of its own. What Golding is saying, I think, is that we project evil onto things that are gruesome and ugly, like a dead pig's head buzzing with flies, but it's a delusion. The pig's head isn't evil. Evil, or the capacity to do evil, is within us and abrupt changes of social circumstance can quickly bring it to the fore.

What I got about *Lord of the Flies* at the age of 14 were the three main characters – Ralph, Jack and Piggy. Ralph, I identified with – I got his dimly understood belief in civilised standards of behaviour, I understood the black shadow of depression that 'flutters' on his brain, so too his faltering sense of reality under escalating stress. Jack, I got at a glance – he's the lead bully. In defence of the old school, however, I do want to say that I never saw a single bully dominate the whole place like Jack did. Not nearly. Nor did I see, as happens in movies (including, I think, the 1963 film version of *Lord of the Flies*), a whole group of kids with a uniform intent of causing hurt. What I saw was a couple causing hurt and, on the faces of the rest, doubt and uncertainty as they realised it would take Jesus Christ to stop what was unfolding before their eyes and Jesus Christ wasn't present.

The character who haunted me was Piggy. The fat kid with glasses who can't run with the pack. There was a kid who looked like my imagining of Piggy at our school in my last year. He was old womanly in manner. He's the one I was told was found about to hang himself in the alcove next to the chapel and the other kid talked him down.

Lord of the Flies ends when a British naval officer is drawn to the island by the fact it's on fire. What he finds is a gang of young savages hunting down one of their number – Ralph – to murder him. They have just murdered Piggy after a hunt *in which Ralph has participated*! Standing among them, the disbelieving officer mutters something to the effect that he thought English boys could have done better. At his feet sits a kid with a grimy face and torn clothes weeping 'for the loss of innocence'. It's Ralph. The black weight has landed.

★

Golding got sick of saying what he thought the book was about, but on one occasion he did say it was about the Rule of Law. As he struggles to create a civilised order, Ralph proposes a boy parliament. The symbol of each boy's right to speak and be heard is a shell they call the conch. Here's a key passage:

> Piggy said, I got the conch.
> Conch! Conch! shouted Jack, We don't need the conch any more. We know who ought to say things … It's time some people knew they've got to keep quiet, and leave deciding things to the rest of us.

It was mid-2020 when I talked to the kids in Gilroye's class. I told the kids, mostly white and Latino, that that's where we were at historically. The Jacks were stealing the conch in my country, in their country, in Britain. The people who will suffer are the Piggys. I refrained from saying I thought Trump was Jack. In seeking to insult Republican Senator John McCain, a prisoner during the Vietnam War who was tortured, Trump said his heroes were people who weren't captured. At this point he revealed himself to have a child's view of war, one no doubt acquired in the safety of a New York cinema. I told them a little about Weary Dunlop.

In 1985, shortly after arriving in Melbourne, I was introduced to the grandson of General Sir John Monash, Jewish-Australian World War I hero. He was decades older than me and had, in the past, reviewed books for *The Age*. I was introduced as a writer. 'What's your favourite novel?' he asked coolly. On impulse, I said *Lord of the Flies*. He replied. 'So you're a depressive, are you?'

Lord of the Flies does represent a depressing view of human nature. What I said to the 14-year-olds is that it's only one view. Want another? Read Mark Twain's *Huckleberry Finn*. Read Abraham Lincoln's second Inaugural Address. William Golding's novel doesn't explain Abraham Lincoln. It doesn't explain Weary Dunlop or Patrick Dodson, it doesn't explain Rinso or Tim, it doesn't explain my wife and lots of other women I've met … life's about balance.

★

Through Newie, I re-met his brother Peter. It was Peter Newport who stopped Jagger's reign of terror in my second year. I can still feel the relief that followed the result of that fight. Peter was only at the old school for two years. His working life was spent as an underground miner until he got vertebrae crushed in a rockfall. He now works as a handyman fixing and inventing things. He was a silent intense kid at school. The man I meet 50-odd years later is talkative and quick of mind with strong opinions. I asked him about the fight with Jagger.

What does he remember of the fight?

He remembers a kid on the side yelling out, 'Hit him, Jagger! Hit him!' He names the kid.

Peter's story accords with what I thought of that kid at the time. He made it his business to be in with the right people – I was wary of him. Then, about five years after school, I met him in Hobart and found him friendly and open and had the surprise of liking him. Neither of us had emerged from the old school innocent. I'll forgive you if you forgive me, that way we start again. I keep meeting people I went to school with who want to start again.

★

Meeting Peter Newport made me think about Jagger, the kid from the orphanage who was stopped in one of the most sensational fights I ever saw. Jagger would be surprised, I think, to know just how well I remember him: the dry red skin on his knuckles, the sensual mouth ... He actually carried himself with a certain Steve McQueen-type physical grace – he had presence and knew it. He was also, by the age of 12, a fighting machine. I say this as someone who has covered two world title fights.

Ah, Jagger, the things we do before we know what we're doing ...

★

The school's 25th anniversary came around in the early 1980s. A lawyer old boy rang me and asked me to write something for the local newspaper advertising the event. I said that as my time at the school had been the worst of my life, that was unlikely. For the school's 50th anniversary, the organiser contacted me personally. He was a fan of my work. Could I please come?

I wanted to help him. I could tell he had a good heart, but I wasn't ready. I had to write something like this book first. There's a Zen saying – 'The Obstacle Is The Way'. This was the obstacle. I had to work out once and for all what it meant to me. And before I went back, there was a fear I'd have to overcome, the fear of meeting people from my time. I'd be thinking they were thinking, 'I don't care what you might have done since you left school, I know who you really are.'

If I was to re-enter that world, I had to do it on my own terms. I had, as it were, to come out.

*

Towards the end of 2018, I heard that a ceremony was being organised for victims of sexual abuse at the old school. I saw a parish newsletter advertising what was termed A Ritual of Lament: 'to acknowledge and remember those who have suffered sexual abuse'. The old school's blue crest sat beside the words, together with, in italics, '*We gather together committed to the healing process and to reconciling our past with our hope for the future.*' RSVPs to be directed through the school.

I was like a plane hitting turbulence. Should I go? I don't like ceremonies – they're too staged. No spontaneity. I don't like religious language in the same way that I don't like political correctness – they assume belief. The big assumption here was that a ritual, however well-intentioned, could genuinely unleash a feeling as deep as lamentation. I fear inauthentic emotion. It repulses me no matter what political angle it comes from. '*We gather together committed to the healing process and to reconciling our past with our hope for the future.*' Religious types seem to think that proclaiming that a gathering will have a certain spirit means it's going to happen. I say something that profound happens rarely and, when it does, it's the product of great storytelling, great film, great theatre.

But, if you go along, you have to play along – to do otherwise would be rude and disrespectful. Better to stay away. But I have to admit: part of me wanted to go for a look. I made a career out of going for a look. But to go in that spirit would be to treat those involved like animals in a zoo. That struck me as gross and I feared going in the wrong spirit – doing it 'wrong way' – as I could end up saying or doing something I regretted. This was going to be a very big day for some people – it would be neither the time nor the place to behave in a petty manner.

To my relief, the March 2020 Ritual of Lament was cancelled because of COVID. Twelve months later, it was back on. By then, I was better prepared. I'd written a draft of this book and had a clearer understanding of what I thought about the whole thing, but I was still put off by the idea of participating in a 'religious' ceremony. Tim couldn't go as he had to be in Brisbane for a medical conference. I was wrestling with it all anew when Newie made the decision simple, as is his gift. He told me he was going and asked me to accompany him. He said, 'I reckon we ought to go and show our support for the blokes it happened to.'

★

'Love the Truth,' says the school motto. Do I? Do I Love the Truth?

On a TV show that explores family histories, I watched a man learn that around the time of World War I his grandfather deserted his grandmother, leaving her in poverty, pregnant and with syphilis. Does the man who learned that about his heritage love the truth? Should he?

Do I love the truth when I learn of atrocities committed on civilian populations, when I see a photo of a Ukrainian child who has lost her mother and both her legs in a Russian rocket attack when Putin is attempting to bash Ukraine into submission? No, what I feel then is a numb paralysis.

I lack what Catholics call faith, which I understand to be an inner assurance that the universe is ultimately just and ordered. What I know is that there is a capacity for love in the world which is reborn in every generation and cannot be extinguished – but I don't see any evidence that it is assured of a final victory and it sure has some demoralising losses along the way. My response, to quote Leonard Cohen, has been 'to ring the bells that still can ring'.

I have a wise friend who talks Catholic theology in a way that makes some sense to me as a philosophy. I asked him about 'Love the Truth' in specific reference to the man who discovered his grandfather had left his pregnant grandmother ill and impoverished. He replied, 'It doesn't say the truth will make you happy, it says the truth will make you free.'

When my friend read the manuscript of this book, he was shocked and said, 'You've got to go back to the school. I'll come with you, if you want.'

★

A voice in my head says, you got away from the old school, you escaped it in your head – why go back again? If you go back, something will happen. You know that because stories are never more powerful than in the places they're from. You're going back to the place where one of your primal stories is from. You think you've dealt with that part of your life, but what if something's revealed to you about yourself that you had forgotten, something that shocks you like Herman shocked you that day when he summoned you from class in First Year and the floor swam beneath your feet.

I repeat to myself a quote of Mahatma Gandhi's, if you do the right thing for the right reason, you'll generally be protected. This can be read as cliché but I believe it contains a valuable wisdom. It involves asking yourself two questions as honestly as you are able: am I doing the right thing, and am I doing it for the right reason? Deceiving yourself at that level can land you in big trouble, but I thought we were going back for the right reason. Like Newie said, we were going for the ones it happened to. I trust Newie like a mountain climber trusts the climber he makes a big ascent with.

A lady rings me three days before the event. She's an aggrieved Catholic. She knows I gave evidence in a court case against a local priest. She knows I'm a journalist. She's full of gossip about priests who have passed through the town where the old school sits, regardless of whether they had anything to do with the school. She cries, 'I'll tell you which child belongs to which priest!' (Can't wait to tell Tim that one!) She wants to meet me at the Ritual, says, 'There are people I can introduce you to,' and I'm saying, 'No thanks, no thanks, NO THANKS.' I'm going for the ones it happened to.

★

The Ritual of Lament is held in a rhododendron park up behind the town. Newie and I arrive to what seems a lot of cars. The event's highly organised – there are plenty of volunteers. It's a broad-based effort, not the work of a few individuals. The service is in a deep gully walled with rhododendron bushes and topped with tall eucalypts. The rhododendrons are not in bloom so the gully is deeply green. At its base is a small lake of black water, a white rotunda and a speaker's podium bearing the blue crest of the old school.

We'd arranged to meet Rinso who had flown down from Sydney. He was one of only two former students to testify against Tom. His interaction with Tom was a one-off. He'd got Rinso to drop his pyjama trousers and tapped his cock to give him an erection, for the stated purpose of seeing that he was 'in good working order'. Over the years, the incident hadn't 'distressed' him, but it was always in the back of his mind. About 10 years ago, he returned to Tasmania for one of his informal school reunions. Of the eight old boys at the table, six admitted to having been 'touched up' by different priests, mostly Tom. 'I thought, "This is shocking ... someone has to do something about it."' He rang a hotline for the Royal Commission into Sexual Abuse. There followed a call from the Tasmanian police.

Rinso told me he was surprised more kids hadn't come forward to testify against Tom. Paul O'Halloran told me he and his brother Steve heard virtually nothing after they did the ABC online story accusing Herman, the former rector and head of the order, of being an abuser. I'm reminded of when I wrote my essay on torture and heard nothing back. Once again I hear in my head T. S. Eliot's dictum that humankind cannot bear too much reality.

Paul and Steve O'Halloran are at the rhododendron park. Pen in hand, Paul's taking notes. My surprise is that there are not more former students, only a dozen or so that I know. School staff with name badges circulate among us. They are friendly and welcoming. From what I can see, the audience are basically local parishioners, mostly elderly people, a remarkable number of whom are wearing white which shines in the sun. The shining white becomes part of my visual memory of the day. A good crowd, maybe 120, the gully seems full.

Taking our seats among some plush foliage on the side, we are informed that a snake lives nearby. The snake will reappear during the ritual, making people leap in the air and look beneath their chairs. There's a lot of laughter. I see the ghosts of Booze and Eric, both now departed, descending upon us like avenging angels, there being no worse crime than laughing when the archbishop, the man who works in God's office, is in attendance. I repel Booze and Eric, saying, 'God laughs. I know – Desmond Tutu told me.'

A young woman in school uniform identifies herself confidently as Aboriginal and does a welcome to country, talking about reconciliation. The school singing group performs from the rotunda. One of their songs, 'Bridge Over Troubled Water', takes me back to 1971, my last year, when I discovered Simon and Garfunkel. The school choir leaves, filing upwards out of the gully. There's this feeling of the young ones having been sent away because adult matters are to be discussed. Something actual's about to happen. It's like in the dormitory at night when the discipline master's door opened and you saw a chunk of yellow light as the next kid was beckoned inside to be caned, and you lay there in the dark listening, awaiting the actuality of pain.

★

In turn, three men stand, their wives beside them. The first lifts me from my seat. Peter Dwyer, a freckled kid with snowy hair and glasses, nickname Peck, finished school the year before I did. He left to become a priest.

To a certain sort of Catholic family, having a son become a priest was as big as it got. Such an individual became part of a blessed elite entrusted with doing God's work on earth, forgiving sins which were further defined as sins against God. Such a man knew bishops, may even have been to the Vatican, the grand palace of Roman Catholicism. In those days a standard photo that used to circulate in Catholic circles was of the young priest in his robes on his ordination day, his parents kneeling in front of him, thereby acknowledging their son's elevation to this higher status of being an instrument of God.

Peter Dwyer's parents were deeply committed Catholics. Now he was returning to his parents' parish, to tell the congregation his experience wasn't at all like their preconception, that before he left for the seminary he was trapped into a sexual relationship with Tom, after he went to Tom's room to ask about becoming a priest. Tom got him to display his 'sexual maturity'.

'I believed his story – that sexual maturity was necessary for such a life.' He returned to Tom's room a number of times. 'I obeyed and trusted a priest. At the end of each session, he would open a drawer and take out his priestly stole, tell me that I had sinned and say that he would hear my confession – I was *wrong*, I had *sinned*. I believed him, I trusted him … and it has been difficult to trust ever since.'

Peter Dwyer was Sir Joseph Porter KCB in the school production of *HMS Pinafore*, a role he played with gusto. He wasn't a gifted actor but he could command the stage and seemed to enjoy doing so. I otherwise knew him as a mild-mannered bespectacled day boy who was good at tennis (I now also know he saw the boarders as 'a rough lot'). The prettiest girl in our sister school would have nothing to do with any of us – it was highly symbolic when she went to a school dance with Peter Dwyer. Peter bought the whole Catholic package. He was a religious innocent. When he read the details of Tom's 2017 court case and realised that Tom's modus operandi was known to the order before he told them, he wept.

★

Afterwards, he will remember his speech that day as a waterfall, a torrent of language rushing from his mouth. It's the first time he's ever spoken in public on the subject and he's not speaking to a like-minded audience at a conference in Melbourne or Sydney. He's speaking in his home town, in what was described for decades as one of the most conservative electorates in Australia.

It's not enough to say you're *born* in your home town. You're *planted* in your home town. You absorb its sights and colours and ways, like shrubs absorb nutrients from the soil. Each town along the coast thinks it's different from the rest, and this one very proudly so. Semi-industrial, it was tougher, harder, as was reflected in the way the two town teams played footy. The kid who threatened me in my first game in the Under 13Bs was the young brother of a local champion.

You know your home town like you know the smell of the factory on the side of town. You swallowed it each time you passed on your way back to school after holidays, and your stomach tightened in a sick way. We can leave our home towns, but they house our memories so that when we come back there's a historical underlay to the visit, a former life follows us around. You think about the person you actually were, as distinct from the person everyone thought you were, or were going to be.

Peter Dwyer's come back. Now they're going to see the other him who grew up in their midst. In what they hold sacred he found profanity. Either he's a liar or he's speaking the truth, the whole truth and nothing but the truth, so help us God.

★

In the green gully, he exclaimed: 'The damage is part of us, not just a feeling. This abuse left me with ongoing feelings of inadequacy and unimportance, of not being good enough, isolated and alone, with mental confusion and disassociation in times of stress, inability to feel love or express it, with emotional and sexual dysfunction. How could I be a husband, a father, a sexual partner, a man?'

His voice rang out: 'How many priests were involved?!' He called out seven names from the order with criminal convictions or serious allegations against them. 'Sometimes I feel as disoriented and vulnerable as I did in that room 50 years ago … I don't know what words I want to hear from the order and I don't think they really know what to say or what to do either.'

He had asked his wife, Rosemary, not to stand too close to him when he spoke, lest her clear-eyed sympathetic presence bring him undone. I watched him after he returned to his seat, how he sat hunched up, the tension within him. His speech had been a mighty effort. It was like he rolled a boulder away from in front of a cave; people looked inside the cave and saw a soul's torment.

★

The second speaker. Kevin O'Sullivan. Born 1971, my last year at the school. His abuse started when he was 14 and lasted until he was 17. The priest is the same Laurie named by John Girdauskas, the one who walked naked through the bush with boys sporting an erection, declaring he wasn't a prude, who didn't like priests who didn't dress like priests (that is, wear a clerical collar), and said the Mass in Latin. The one who visited us in Rosebery. Mum cooked tea. Dad was interested in his talk of Japan, from where he had recently returned after years as a missionary.

Laurie befriended Kevin's parents. His father was a police prosecutor. In later life, his father confronted Laurie but couldn't get him to confess. Laurie was confident, seducing the son of a policeman. John Girdauskas' relationship with Laurie lasted four years. Kevin O'Sullivan's lasted three, finishing when he was 17.

At the age of 18, serving overseas with the RAAF, he wore his Catholicism with pride 'and felt strongly God's call with me'. He also thought he was a fake, and feared being exposed – it would destroy his parents. Suicide came close. Now an officer in the Royal Australian Air Force, Kevin is tautly built with the clear, forthright demeanour of a military man. Today is about direct talk, he says.

'To say it as it is.'

★

Kevin O'Sullivan reminds me of a novel I tried to write. It was about an old footballer in his 40s, someone who could've had a brilliant career but didn't. I started writing it before I testified at Greg's trial, but when that whole drama reappeared in my life I thought why not feed something of it into the novel. I ended up with a character I didn't know and a story I couldn't finish.

The central character's name was Danny. His sexual encounters with a priest lead to a night of gay sex with another boy in the priest's circle. When the other boy gets bashed for being a 'poofter', Danny watches and does nothing. Thirty years later, the other boy goes to the police and lodges a complaint against the priest. The police contact Danny. Danny's still a bit of a name. Troubled career but remembered as a talent. Now living alone but with a reputation from his playing days for wild promiscuity with women. Will he testify?

★

Kevin reads from notes: 'We are often conditioned to see sexual abuse as violent ... it's more often a complicity gained through loyalty and the violation is experienced as tender, seductive and arousing sexual play ... I never felt scared or strange.'

★

You know when you're hearing truth. It's like a chill wind blows through you and everything else becomes silent and still. No-one in the audience moves or murmurs. These people grew up believing in the Holy Roman Catholic Church, as their parents did before them and their parents did before them and so on, as far back as anyone could see. Now they are being told by one of their own that the One, Holy, Catholic and Apostolic Church came with a shadow fashioned in its own image.

Peter Dwyer's emotion was visible throughout his speech. Kevin O'Sullivan is contained but a couple of his pauses are longer than the rest.

★

He says oversexualisation at a young age leaves individuals 'hardwired'. 'The ritual masturbation becomes a pattern and a way that, as a young adolescent, I was able to unconsciously recreate the process of my abuse. It has affected me in all aspects of my maturation.' He says pornography is 'a place we go to seek a salve for our anxiety'.

How many men, with their wives standing beside them, have you heard speak frankly in this way? The answer, in my case, is none.

When he reached adulthood, 'I felt attracted to both females and males, but I knew I was a little bit more attracted to males. I wanted to be heterosexual, I wanted to be normal. I felt that I was morally wrong and I felt the shame … the theology of sin and the need for redemption further messed with my head.'

He's now an air force chaplain. He later wrote to me, 'In my own work, I often experience those in crisis, and journey with them as they try to refind meaning and purpose. I get a strong sense that we are story and when our story has been disrupted we sometimes bury our story, or need to tell that story until we regain our way … I hoped that through telling my story it may provide permission to others that they could also tell their story. I think my life experiences have strengthened my ability to hear others and to offer a more hospitable, welcoming and non-judgemental approach to how I reflect the sacredness of each individual person.'

If I was a young man going through the sort of crisis I went through in my mid-20s, when I was scared out of my existential wits, Kevin would be someone I think I could talk to. He's like Archie Roach and Bob Brown – he's been to the bottom, to realising no-one can help you, that you have no choice, you have to be who you are. I've been there, too.

★

The third speaker, Greg Lehman, is a university professor. He looks like a Viennese psychoanalyst and possesses a gracious intellect. He is also a member of the Tasmanian Aboriginal community in which heated issues of identity arise daily. In that turbulent realm he is calm, and this day he is calm also, saying, 'My desire today is to simply share some of my story as it is. It isn't to bring to you any burden of guilt.'

Lehman outlined his abuse at the hands of former trainee priest Paul G___, who was employed by the school as an athletics coach in the late 1970s and '80s and was jailed for sexual offences against 20 boys aged between 13 and 17 years old in 2005. 'Many of these were students at [the old school]. Many were classmates of mine. Some are still among my closest friends. Some have passed away, including through suicide.'

But Lehman pointedly dedicated his speech to Father Paul Cooney, the head of the order running the school in 2010, when Lehman wrote to him about G___. Cooney quickly got in touch. 'He allowed me to find long overdue peace and grace by his listening and acting. He needed very few words and I thank him for that. But the words he did use were sincere, compassionate, purposeful and accountable ... I was able to forgive G___ before he died. And with this I finally regained some of the grace that was lost to me thirty years ago.'

Greg Lehman brings grace to the day.

The bishop then spoke, followed by the head of the order and the present school principal. The three speakers seemed sincere in expressing their sorrow and regret. That's how Rinso heard it. He was 'overcome'. It was like his father's funeral, he later said. 'I was alright until someone said "Sorry" and put a hand on my shoulder.'

Rinso fought the school bully, got bashed and thought he won. He had the courage to make a stand by testifying against Tom. He started the process of bringing us back together. His is the name at the top of my school honour board.

★

I judge any performance by the spirit left in its wake. The spirit in the aftermath of the speeches and responses was like the excitement in a footy change-room after a big win. Everybody met and mingled. There was tea, coffee, sandwiches, cake. Three priests from my time, old men now, had travelled from interstate.

I congratulated each of the speakers and asked a few questions. It seems a past principal, Adrian Drane, agreed 'Something had to be done' and appointed a committee. The driving forces on the committee were John Girdauskas and Kevin O'Sullivan. It all made sense. That's why the ceremony worked – the pair knew all sides of the experience and were determined to push to a meaningful conclusion. I cannot speak for others, but for me the day resurrected some hope that deep truths can be uttered and heard, that we can move beyond clichés of thought and emotion to the realm of naked humanity.

I'm not sure the event can be replicated. As Paul O'Halloran said to me, 'Even when people say they give everything, they always hold something back. Those blokes held nothing back.' I don't believe many people can bare their primal wound in public. And more than that, in their home town.

A woman with a kind face introduced herself. It turned out she was a reader of mine. We'd been corresponding for years but never met. She took me to another warm, welcoming older woman, the mother of a notable AFL personality. Women elders being there mattered to me. What happened at the school was an all-male affair, yang twisting in on itself. This day has a river of yin flowing through it.

This day I love the truth.

★

Most mornings, around 11, my old schoolmate – *nothing* – appears. To borrow a famous quote, life seems weary, stale, flat and unprofitable. Usually something I read in the news sets me off on a downward trajectory. The feeling intensifies until, around 2 pm, it becomes so unbearable I start writing. That's how I escape nothing. I seek out stories, no matter how local or apparently minor, that, in the immortal words of English poet D. J. Enright, convey 'such courage and wisdom as the race has painfully acquired'.

I don't believe I ever flinched from the horror – for example, the issue of torture – but the reason the horror didn't overwhelm me was because journalism kept sending me out into the world and, in so many unexpected ways, the world has proved better than I imagine it to be. I sought to honour that by finding stories which, to quote Desmond Tutu, could 'withstand the harsh scrutiny of history'.

In 2019, I was asked back to the town where the old school stands to persuade kids to stick with education. What a dazzling irony! The happiest day of my school life was when I ran away and hitchhiked to Hobart and the world fell open before me like a wonderful book.

A contingent of kids, six or so, came from the old school. I get a buzz out of young people. I got a special buzz out of those young people. They were wearing the same blue uniform I wore, I knew the classrooms they sat in on top of that lonely hill, the stretch of sea they looked out on which is mostly grey.

These kids were sensitive to the school's past, like people who live in a haunted house are sensitive to stories about ghosts said to live there. When I said something big happened to me at the old school when I was 13, a nervous laugh ran among them. They thought they knew what had happened, but they didn't. I wanted to tell them, but I wanted to tell them the whole story, I wanted to tell them what I've written in this book.

Plus I wanted to tell them something else besides, something I got from a friend who went to a quiet Catholic school in Melbourne and then experienced the bloody tumult of the civil war in El Salvador. She has a saying, 'Whichever way you go, you meet your Waterloo.'

What does that mean? In my case, it means I was always going to be shocked to the core by life at some point or, more truthfully, at various points along the way. If it hadn't happened at school, it would have happened somewhere else. For some of my genera-tion, it happened in the jungles of Vietnam, fighting a war that an ever-growing number of Australians didn't believe in. I never had to fight in a war. For that and much else, I am deeply grateful. I'd also want to tell those young people something Patrick Dodson wrote inside the cover of one of my books: 'The struggle never ends – the reward is the people you meet along the way.'

Sooner or later, I'll run into someone who doesn't like what I've written. To some, my perspective will be misplaced – it will be like a movie where the camera is pointed in the wrong direction, at the wrong faces. But my perspective is my story. Anyone shaped by such places has a story in them as deep as a novel.

★

In April 2022, with the manuscript of this book approaching completion, I wrote to the three speakers at the Ritual of Lament – Peter Dwyer, Kevin O'Sullivan and Greg Lehman – to tell them I had written a book about the old school that climaxed with the Ritual and their speeches. I didn't require their permission as the event had been open to the media and reported in detail, plus a video of the day's proceedings had been posted on YouTube. But they needed to know about the book since it could bring them renewed public attention and I offered to show them the manuscript. I received replies from Kevin and Greg but not from Peter. A month or so later, I heard Peter was ill with prostate cancer.

On 9 October 2022, I received an email from Peter. It read, in part, 'Health has been a struggle. Last week decided no further chemo. The body isn't up to it. To be honest, it was expected and a relief. We are now focusing on "quality of life" and an array of visits from palliative care team but as yet with no timelines … I don't know what is going faster, the cancer or the decrease of my reading rate but would like to read the manuscript if possible …'

I promptly forwarded the manuscript and said that, if he wished to write a few words, I would put them at the end of the book. A few days later, Peter forwarded the following statement. He starts it in the immediate aftermath of the Ritual of Lament when everybody came together and started talking:

> Laden with speech notes, coffee, sangers and a sausage roll I struggled to understand the conversation I was having with a priest (of the order that ran the school) who attended the Ritual of Lament. And yes the conversation turned immediately to football. But I had just unleashed a waterfall of words to people who were there because they cared. Nothing had happened. Then, or later, no priest from the order acknowledged my words. And only one later in writing, who had watched on line.

He later told me there were other people struck speechless by what he said that day. That would be part of the price he had to pay – that when he finally got it out, when he finally laid himself bare, some of his audience would be unable to speak. Like on 9/11, after two buildings no-one thought could be attacked by air were reduced to rubble by an air attack – that scale of shock, only on a wholly individual basis. Thankfully, there were people there that day who had no difficulty finding words or recognising the reality he described – the ones who'd been at the old school with him as kids, whose stories intersected with his own.

He finished:

Thank you, Martin, Rinso, Tony (Newport), Paul (O'Halloran), Stephen (O'Halloran) and of course John Girdauskas for rescuing me that day and later for telling me what had happened to my words. To Martin in particular for this story of 'the old school' and to John Girdauskas for his selfless Christian commitment.

Martin Flanagan was born in 1955 and graduated in law from the University of Tasmania in 1975. He has written many books, a play and two film treatments. From 1985 to 2017, he wrote for the Melbourne *Age* on sport and other subjects.

What people have said about Martin Flanagan's football writing:

> 'Martin Flanagan must never be allowed to stop writing football. I say this because he is the only football writer I have read who is so good I think he could nearly describe a heartbeat – and that, if you want to touch the essence of football, is what you have to do.' *Don Watson*

> 'The best of Flanagan has a finesse and feeling that no current Australian sports-writer approaches, let alone equals.' *Gideon Haigh*

> 'I love his brain.' *Kevin Sheedy*